Orientations

James Winston Morris

Orientations

ISLAMIC THOUGHT IN A WORLD CIVILISATION

Archetype

This first English language edition published in 2004 by
Archetype
Chetwynd House, Bartlow
Cambridge CB1 6PP, UK
www.archetype.uk.com
Distributed by Central Books Ltd., 99 Wallis Road, London E9 5LN
www.centralbooks.co.uk
In the US distributed by Midpoint Trade Books
www.midpointtradebooks.com

ISBN 1-901383-10-5

British Library Cataloguing in Publication Data
A catalogue record for this book is available from
The British Library

Typeset in Minion by Ian Abdullateef Whiteman / CWDM
Arabic/Farsi typesetting by Decotype, Amsterdam

Cover photograph 'Sunrise, Pokhara, Nepal' copyright © 1985 Eric Lawton.
All rights reserved. www.ericlawtonphotography.com

Printed and bound in Great Britain by St Edmundsbury Press, Bury St Edmunds.

For the peoples of every Jerusalem and Sarajevo

بِسْمِ ٱللَّهِ ٱلرَّحْمَٰنِ ٱلرَّحِيمِ * وَٱلْعَصْرِ * إِنَّ ٱلْإِنسَٰنَ لَفِى خُسْرٍ

* إِلَّا ٱلَّذِينَ ءَامَنُوا۟ وَعَمِلُوا۟ ٱلصَّٰلِحَٰتِ وَتَوَاصَوْا۟ بِٱلْحَقِّ وَتَوَاصَوْا۟ بِٱلصَّبْرِ *

(Sura *al-ʿAsr*, 13 : 1-3)

ز گریه مردم چشمم نشسته در خونست

ببین که در طلبت حال مردمان چونست

(Hafez, *Dīvān*)

CONTENTS

Preface & Acknowledgements

بِسْمِ ٱللَّهِ ٱلرَّحْمَٰنِ ٱلرَّحِيمِ * وَٱلْعَصْرِ * إِنَّ ٱلْإِنسَٰنَ لَفِى خُسْرٍ

* إِلَّا ٱلَّذِينَ ءَامَنُوا۟ وَعَمِلُوا۟ ٱلصَّٰلِحَٰتِ وَتَوَاصَوْا۟ بِٱلْحَقِّ وَتَوَاصَوْا۟ بِٱلصَّبْرِ *

In the Name of God, the All-Loving, the All-Compassionate
By the ending day!
Surely the human being is in rending loss,
Except for those who have true faith and do what is fitting,
and who encourage each other in Truth-and-Right,
and who encourage each other in persevering-in-faith.

(Qur'an, 103: 1-3)

THOSE ALREADY AT home with the Arabic of this Sura will soon recognise that everything else in this book is simply a brief commentary on all that it conveys. But for the others, a few further words of explanation may be helpful.

This Sura's accepted title, and the key word in the divine oath of its opening line, is *al-ʿaṣr*. For a variety of reasons, translators usually employ the most prosaic meaning of that multi-faceted term: the 'late afternoon', or that fading part of each day when we naturally stop, take stock of what has been accomplished, and hopefully contemplate just what can still be completed, the actions that are *now* most fitting and appropriate (our own *ṣāliḥāt*) in the few hours that remain to us. For many, and most understandably, that is also an obligatory time of daily prayer. Apart from that the *ʿaṣr* is also, and just as immediately and naturally, our 'age', our 'epoch', our own critical and decisive moment—our *kairos*—in the long apparent flow of earthly time. And finally, most deeply and closest to the actual root meaning of the Arabic, the original verbal-noun *ʿaṣr* actually refers to the wrenching, twisting and transforming process of literally *pressing out*—from olives, grapes, sugar cane, or a life—its essential, life-giving elixir, while its dregs are thrown into the fire.

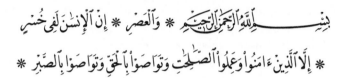

So these three meanings refer to different aspects and dimensions of that same cosmic, yet utterly individual process of *refinement* or transforming purification. And no one who has lived very long needs to be told what is meant by this 'pressing', what comes in its wake, and why and how it leaves so much of each of us in a grievous 'dilemma', in an initially painful state of rending 'loss' and apparent 'damage' (the Qur'anic expression *khusr* here).

But this is only the start of our process. The rest of the Sura is about how the fully, truly human being (*insān*, not the mortal, human-animal *bashar* we all begin with)[1] can and does eventually emerge from that pressing. Hopefully the rest of this book will suggest some of the ways a few of the greatest Islamic thinkers can teach us to carry on this unavoidable purification, discovering and practically applying the four equally essential elements mentioned at the end of this Sura: genuine faith; right action; co-operation in discovering what is Real and Right (*al-Ḥaqq*); and that spiritual community which is indispensable for anyone who would consciously persevere in that right direction in the midst of all of life's recurrent trials of pain and loss. For the ʿ*aṣr* is also that time of day when our directions, in relation to the sun's light, naturally become clear again, the necessary time for re-orientation.

When I was first asked to lecture in Sarajevo—the lectures from which this book emerged—this Sura immediately came to mind. For that invitation immediately brought back indelible memories of a period (1992-93) when the long martyrdom of Sarajevo and so many Bosnian towns and cities was, as it turned out, as yet only beginning and when so many of us were forced to watch helplessly, night after night, unforgettable images of unimaginable horror and suffering, while those who could have intervened and stopped that horror did nothing, or less than nothing. Few forms of torture, of *khusr*, could be more intense than being forced to watch helplessly, at a distance, the repeated martyrdom of entirely innocent people.

Then the ensuing years brought other trials and equally painful reminders, closer to home, of the endless and recurrent forms of

[1] This basic contrast is fundamental throughout the Qur'an, and to all three of our teachers below.

pressing that human beings continue to inflict on each other, experiences of other 'civil wars'. And with time, the initial naïve protestations of 'never again' first crumbled, then slowly gave way—with constant help and guidance from our chosen authors and other companions along that particular path—to a slowly dawning recognition of the wider realities and deeper purposes of this pressing-house's unavoidable 'again and again'. And as that happened, this Sura with which we began was mysteriously joined by an equally fitting and illuminating verse from Hafez. The timeless Persian poems of that true 'guardian of secrets', as people have rediscovered again and again for many centuries, have all the healing and transforming power of divine speech.

So his concluding line of our dedication can be literally translated as follows:

From the weeping of people, my eyes are filled with suffering
('sitting in blood')
See how in their seeking You, what the state of the peoples has
become!

Hafez's secret, of course, is entirely contained in his *vision*, in that transformed perspective he invites us to discover for ourselves, through each of his ghazals. His anguished—yet liberating—cry of '*See!*' is directed at the same time to each of us, and also to his only Beloved, Who is addressed here directly in the second-person singular, in that most impossibly intimate *you*—no longer as 'He' or '*Hū*' or 'God' or any other of the countless divine Names of Beauty and of Majesty.

All the secrets of our sages are already contained in Hafez's infinitely revealing *you*. Each of these thinkers offers us a new orientation, a new 'way of seeing', and attempts to orient us in the direction of that Light. There are endlessly different ways of speaking of that same journey: from the 'Fire' to the 'Gardens'; from blindness to immediate vision (*ru'ya*); from seeking to 'finding' and true Being (*wujūd*); from outer appearances to what is most inner (*al-bāṭin*); of the unveiling of what is purposefully hidden; from the repeated cycles of nature and history to the timeless spiralling ascension (*miʿrāj*) of the perfected soul; and from the outward forms of all revelation to true proximity to God (*walāya*).

Yet all those voyages and paths, and the culminating journey of 'return' as well, are already foreshadowed—here and now, in the tumultuous midst of this only too visible 'Pressing'—in the ineffable, yet ever-present reality of Hafez's incomparably simple *you*.

*

The initial impetus for this book was due to Dr. Hafiz Nevad Kahteran, of the Faculty of Philosophy at the University of Sarajevo, who invited me to give the series of lectures from which this book emerged, under the sponsorship of the Faculty of Philosophy and the Faculty of Islamic Sciences in Sarajevo. He was also instrumental in arranging for the Bosnian translation and original publication of these essays in book form, thanks above all to the energetic support of the director of the El-Kalem Press, Professor Dr. Muhamed Mrahorović. He also prevailed on his able colleagues, Professor Rešid Hafižović and Professor Adnan Siladjzić, both of the Faculty of Islamic Sciences, to share the burdens of translation; the challenges of their task can well be imagined by anyone familiar with the unique style and density of al-Fārābī and Ibn ʿArabī, in particular. My special thanks are due to all those welcoming individuals and institutions, and to their colleagues and families in Bosnia, who actually made those lectures possible.

The contents and form of this book are the fruit of almost three decades of studying, teaching and constantly learning from each of the three thinkers I discuss here, along with many other related figures in the intellectual and spiritual traditions to which they belong. So it would take not just many pages, but many books, simply to mention and adequately thank all those teachers, friends, guides, and often unknowing 'masters' who helped to dramatise and bring those teachings to life. Truly there is no better training ground for adequately translating and communicating unfamiliar writers or traditions than having to teach them to students, of all ages and backgrounds, innocent of any previous familiarity with their work, languages and cultural context. So particular thanks are due to the many hundreds of students, both graduate and undergraduate—in London and Paris, Princeton, Temple, Oberlin, and most recently at

Exeter—who over the years have so constantly and unselfishly taught me again and again how to read, understand and gradually to live and share the teachings introduced in this book.

The growing world-wide interest in these three thinkers, grounded in the tangible relevance and immediate importance of their teachings in our contemporary circumstances for seekers coming from every religious and cultural tradition, is certainly quite visible in the recent profusion of international seminars, conferences, colloquia and workshops devoted to the elaboration and communication of their ideas—especially in the cases of Ibn ʿArabī and Ostad Elahi. In particular, during the self-consciously 'millennial' period immediately preceding the Sarajevo lectures, I was initially encouraged to develop many of the ideas and themes eventually elaborated in this book in several public lectures, including one on Ostad Elahi at a colloquium on the theme of 'ethics and spirituality' at the Ecole normale supérieure in Paris (thanks to Dr. Elie During and the Fondation O. Elahi); on related themes in Islamic eschatology at Oxford University's Centre for Islamic Studies (thanks to Professor Y. Michot); and on Ibn ʿArabī in a particularly fruitful international conference at the University of Kyoto, as well as at the International Symposium of the Muhyiddīn Ibn ʿArabī Society held that year in Chisholme, Scotland.

The first place I was able to outline these themes all together was in my Inaugural Lecture at the University of Exeter, and this book would not have been possible without the extraordinarily supportive circumstances and encouragement so kindly provided by that exceptional University and my colleagues at its promising new Institute of Arab and Islamic Studies. Finally, nothing at all would have been possible without the knowing presence of my wife Corey and—my dearest teachers!—all our children.

James W. Morris
Exeter, 2003

INTRODUCTION

Orientations: Discovering the Process and Tasks of 'Realisation'

وَلِلَّهِ ٱلْمَشْرِقُ وَٱلْمَغْرِبُ ۚ فَأَيْنَمَا تُوَلُّوا۟ فَثَمَّ وَجْهُ ٱللَّهِ ۚ

God's is the place-of-shining-forth and the place-of-darkening: so wherever you-all turn around, then there is the Face of God!

(Qur'an, 2:115)

THE CLASSICAL THINKERS and teachers of any civilisation are enduring, in the end, not because of the striking form of their words, or the particular truths and doctrines they might articulate—all of which age and become more remote as time passes—but because can they still turn us toward a Reality (Arabic: *al-Ḥaqq*) which is immediately present. This book is not intended as either a summary or even an adequate introduction to any of the three thinkers whose works are discussed below. Its focus, instead, is on the recurrent human tasks and challenges which they can help illuminate, even today. The purpose of these essays is to suggest how these teachers can turn our attention toward those *universal* elements of Islamic thought and spirituality which are explicitly grounded in recurrent dimensions of human experience, with the hope that they may help provide us with indispensable foundations for real communication. For without real communication, they remind us, we cannot hope to create a true community, a community based on lasting cultural creativity and individual and collective realisation and transformation, in that global civilisation which is so rapidly coming into being all around and through us. Their common starting point—and their ultimate conclusions—are beautifully articulated in the celebrated verse above, whose depths have only too often been betrayed by inadequate translation.

That verse begins, as our three subjects do, with what we all already know simply as human beings, immediately and spontaneously, at every point of our lives, without any further reference or explanation, certainly without any particular religious or theological beliefs. No one needs to be told, at any moment, what is our own particular *mashriq*, our own place or direction of relative illumination, of the 'dawning light'. And even less do we need any hints about our own 'places of darkening' (*maghrib*), of the fading of that same light. That initial, existential orientation, with all its shifting dilemmas and predicaments, is built into our existence from infancy to death, and it never leaves us. We may delude ourselves, of course, and often do. But the roots of all authentic learning, of all spiritual discernment and transformation, begin with that possibility of delusion and with its resulting revelation of ever deeper lights and sources of direction.

Orientation implies direction and movement. So the verse goes on to remind us that we are all[2] constantly engaged in two very different sorts of 'turning around'. Most obviously and naturally, from the fading toward the dawning light, from memory and its obsessions toward what is newly, potentially coming to be. But also, as we all discover quickly enough, we are only too frequently turning *away* from what is truly Light (*al-nūr*: the 'true Sun' shared by both these places of true dawning and dusk), toward a multitude of glimmering, illusory lights which are eventually exposed as such by their memorably painful quality of purifying 'fire' (*al-nār*). Can this verse really be saying that there too, even when we turn away in so many wrong directions, we are still discovering the 'Face of God'?

In one objective, ontological sense, that is certainly already and always the case. For the larger context of the Qur'an refers repeatedly to all the qualitative aspects of manifest being and our experience as ultimately rooted in a vast spectrum of divine Names (qualities or attributes) which initially appear to us as polar opposites: for example as the contrasting experiences of 'Beauty' and terrible 'Majesty', of immanence and unimaginable transcendence (or as yin and yang).[3] In that sense, certainly, we can *only* see the shifting faces and

[2] The 'you' here is pointedly in the general *plural*: everyone is addressed by this mysterious Speaker.

[3] The familiar theological categories of divine *jamāl* and *jalāl*, of *tashbīh* and *tanzīh*.

ever-changing aspects of a reality whose true nature and deeper purpose we can only intuit. To use Ibn ʿArabī's powerful expression, we cannot help imagining and all do surmise some 'god' (some hypothetical source of all these shifting faces)—but we are far from really knowing that all those relative lights really are one Light, or that their source truly is *All-Loving* and *infinitely Compassionate* (*al-Raḥmān*). So at first any orientation we might discover from this divine comedy will understandably seem provisional and shaky at best.

But the wider Qur'anic context (and helpful philologians) also make it clear that the 'Face' mentioned here (*wajh*: the Arabic also means 'direction' and 'heading') also has the deeper meaning of the *essential reality* of a thing, and thus of the underlying Reality and Essence behind this ever-turning play of admitted darkness and relative light. This is the mystery expressed in the familiar but unfathomed word that opens and closes this verse, and in the equally mysterious Voice that addresses us here in Its Name. That next, deeper level of orientation is where each of our three guides begins.

THE PROCESS OF REALISATION

The universality of this predicament and the process of orientation to which it gives rise have been classically expressed in two interrelated Arabic expressions—*al-Ḥaqq* and *taḥqīq*—which we begin with here simply because they so economically summarise the subject of this book and the common purposes uniting these otherwise very different teachers. To begin with, the term *al-Ḥaqq* refers both to what is truly real and to what is right, obligatory and fair. In other words, this 'truly Real'—for it is the most all-encompassing of the divine Names—is at once the ultimate Reality, absolute Truth,[4]

[4] Precisely in the sense of what is absolutely, incontrovertibly Real. We have only mentioned this very particular sense of 'the Truth' here because it is so commonly found in English translations from the Arabic. In fact, as we have learned to our dismay from many years of teaching, it is basically impossible in English to utter or read the word 'truth' without immediately and unavoidably suggesting a whole complex mental web of inseparably related meanings and assumptions about beliefs, falsehood, untruths, proofs, etc.—all of which are utterly absent from, and indeed completely contradictory to, the actual semantic field of this particular Arabic expression in its Qur'anic usage and in most writings drawn from and referring to that Qur'anic context. In all those contexts, *ḥaqq* is the Reality that one finds (*wujūd*)—not something people need to prove, defend, etc.—and

and Right. Thus, and inseparably from that Reality (an inseparability entirely lost in English translations!), it is the vast complex of human and divine rights and responsibilities that flow from our recognition of the Real, at whatever level and context that recognition may take place.[5] The second, derivative expression, *taḥqīq*, is simply the 'action of finding-and-making real' whatever we know to be *ḥaqq*. Thus *taḥqīq* means the inseparably moral, spiritual and intellectual tasks of both discovering and investigating—and then concretely actualising or 'making real'—everything that is demanded of us by that *ḥaqq* we are striving to know. Therefore it again encompasses a recurrent human experience which we normally tend to express (and perhaps even to think of) in English as two or three quite distinct processes. First, there is our gradual discovery or 'realisation' (and eventual 'verification') of what *is* actually real and obligatory for us, the slow awakening of spiritual discernment. Only then can we effectively undertake the responsibilities and the ongoing challenges—necessarily both individual and communal—of communication, actualisation, realisation and transformation which are always needed in order to bring those real principles of *ḥaqq* into actual existence in ourselves and others. So in time, the process of *taḥqīq* appears as, and entails, these three indispensable elements: consciousness, communication, and community.

Each of our three guides and thinkers[6] here has dealt with all the stages and dimensions of that process of realisation and actualisation in powerfully revealing and lastingly influential ways. But each one also has certain characteristic focuses, concentrations and distinctive forms of expression which make them particularly useful for contemporary readers in specific domains and different practical contexts and situations. Al-Fārābī, as a self-consciously and explicit-

---

the concomitant Right or obligation which one immediately knows, and therefore must also do or actualise ('make real').

[5] Humanly speaking, of course, we more often move from the awakened conscience, from our immediate awareness of what is right, to a deeper consciousness of its Source and its wider spiritual implications. That natural, everyday movement from ethics to spirituality is the focus of our discussion of Ostad Elahi's spiritual pedagogy in Chapter Three below.

[6] Or better, our *muḥaqqiqūn*, the classical Arabic expression for all those who undertake and realise all these intrinsic demands of *taḥqīq*.

ly rational philosopher, focuses above all on our social and political existence and on what we can know and must ultimately accomplish in that worldly context. Thus I begin with him and the common human tasks of clear-sightedness and communication which are so central to his writing and teaching. Ibn ʿArabī's concerns are so wide (and his writings so prolific) that it is difficult to typify him in any way at all. But his greatest book, *al-Futūḥāt al-Makkīya*, is an incomparable collection of universal spiritual 'illuminations'. And he is undoubtedly (among many other things) one of humanity's most lastingly effective and influential guides to our unfolding development of spiritual insight, and to the ever-wider responsibilities and possibilities of creativity and transformation which flow from every true inspiration. Finally, the culminating stages of realisation and human perfection, in every tradition, demand the constant synthesis and active integration of the outer and the inner worlds, of what might initially appear to many of us as two very different paths of reason and spiritual insight. Few proponents of that integrated human vision, of the tasks and responsibilities of 'spiritual intelligence', have been so clearly articulate and immediately accessible as the remarkable recent Iranian thinker and teacher Ostad Elahi, whose understanding of the central role of spirituality in everyone's everyday life—a particularly relevant emphasis in this emerging global civilisation—is the focus of our third chapter below.

'STAYING *REAL*': CONTEXT AND DISCOVERY

With each of these three authors, as with any great philosopher or spiritual teacher, it is only too easy to get lost in their words, symbols and concepts. This can happen at any stage, depending on our mental and spiritual particularities and surrounding circumstances. Whenever that does happen—and each of these authors has their own distinctive ways of recalling us to the realities at hand, of bringing their readers back 'down to earth'—it is sufficient, and certainly necessary, for us to return to the actual context and immediate problems and dilemmas of our own existence, whether those are apparently within or outside us. What these figures have to teach us can only really be grasped in those constantly changing concrete, personal contexts. And that actualised spiritual intelligence which is their common aim can only be discovered and maintained through those very real and inescapable challenges whose forms, providentially enough, are always 'tutorials' exquisitely tailored to our own uniquely individual learning needs.

This constant practical necessity of 'getting real'—to use the telling colloquial expression—is just as true whether we are starting with the first half of realisation, the initial task of discovering what is truly real and right; or whether we are beginning with the continuation and completion of that discovery in a particular newly unfolding responsibility of communication and transformation. In either case, the deeper human cycle of *taḥqīq* and realisation is always the same, epitomised in both our opening Qur'anic verse (of this chapter) and in the dedicatory Sura *al-'aṣr*: first comes the predicament (*al-ᶜaṣr*, the 'time of darkening'), the irresolvable dilemma or the epiphanic moment of marvel and mystery—what Ibn ᶜArabī calls the divine gift of 'bewilderment' (*ḥayra*). Then the resulting seeking, the 'turning around' for light and genuine resolution, a time and a task which can seem desperately interminable.[7] And finally (or so we always imagine), the always miraculous instant of surrender, grace and illumination—that ineffable 'opening'[8] which, whenever we hold on to it, soon becomes another painful pitfall and obsession. Then comes the discovery of our next task, and the process begins again.

The problem, of course, is that we only too quickly become familiar with this cycle, and with the key educational roles of ignorance, failure and half-hearted approximation. Those particular lifelong lessons are painful and demanding enough, each time around, that we are always easy prey for all the variegated natural avoidance mechanisms of distraction, heedlessness, or entertaining escape into the fascinating realms of theory, concepts and symbols divorced from those

[7] Hence the recurring emphasis in our last two teachers below, as in the Sura of *al-ᶜAṣr*, on the practical centrality of inner faith (*īmān*) and illumined perseverance, *ṣabr*.

[8] The literal—and so phenomenologically appropriate—meaning of that technical Sufi term (*fatḥ*; pl. *futūḥāt*) which provides the title and essential subject of Ibn 'Arabi's magnum opus, usually translated in this study (to accord with the published versions) as *The Meccan Illuminations*.

actual realities. When any of those habitual mechanisms kick in, each of our teachers, in their own way, is quick to remind us that *taḥqīq* is not a mental or intellectual process, nor a technique which we can somehow finish learning and then simply choose to apply from time to time—that the construction of our fully human community, and the communication that alone can ever bring that reality into our being, is a work that has always only just begun...

*

We have just spoken of a 'cycle', but the word 'task' in each of our chapter titles is a practical reminder that this process is actually a gradually ascending spiral (*miʿrāj*), never a pointless repetition, once we have actually begun to learn *how* to learn.[9] The true Teacher in question, and the exact length of our private lessons in realisation, are beautifully expressed in the following equally famous Qur'anic verse. Each of our three guides reveals some of its secrets.

سَنُرِيهِمْ ءَايَٰتِنَا فِى ٱلْءَافَاقِ وَفِىٓ أَنفُسِهِمْ حَتَّىٰ يَتَبَيَّنَ لَهُمْ أَنَّهُ ٱلْحَقُّ ۗ

We shall continue to show them ('*cause them to see*') *Our Signs on the horizons and in their own souls until it becomes clear* ('*shines forth*') *to them that Hū*[10] *is the truly Real* (*al-Ḥaqq*)...

(from the Sura *Fuṣṣilat*, 41:53)

[9] The allusion here is to Ibn ʿArabī's characteristic emphasis on the central Qur'anic teaching of the 'ever-renewed creation' of all existence at every instant and to his equally characteristic insistence (even more forcefully reiterated by Ostad Elahi, in Chapter Three below) that the truly *complete* spiritual journey, as exemplified by each of the divine Messengers and prophets, is not some spiritual departure from this world, but integrally includes the transforming task of 'return', only this time 'by and with God'.

[10] Retaining the actual Arabic divine Name—which is anything but a pronoun, much less of any specific gender—here and in its other frequent Qur'anic contexts (rather than the usual English translation as 'He') is at least one partially effective way of conveying that the reference here is to the ultimate, all-encompassing divine Essence, to what is most Real, Present and Absolute, not at all to any sort of abstraction or concept or absent reality. This expression is traditionally the Islamic equivalent of the 'unspeakable' divine Name in other Abrahamic religious traditions.

CHAPTER ONE

Toward a Community of Ends: al-Fārābī and the Tasks of Clarity and Communication

اَللّٰهُمَّ أَرِنَا ٱلأَشْيَاءَ كَمَا هِيَ

O my God, cause us to see things as they really are.

PRAYER OF THE PROPHET

But in heaven, perhaps a pattern is laid up for the person who wants to see and found a city within himself on the basis of what he sees. It doesn't make any difference whether it is or will be somewhere. For he would mind the things of this city alone, and of no other.[11] *REPUBLIC*, BOOK IX

FOR SOME ACADEMIC philosophers, the recurrent emphasis on happiness throughout al-Fārābī's writings[12] might seem a sort of superficial rhetorical device, designed to draw curious

[11] For those unfamiliar with the *Republic*, it may be helpful to recall the larger context of Socrates' words here at the end of Book IX, just before the concluding 'myth of Er'. Plato, in the middle of Book II, has his actors turn from the consideration of justice in the individual, in the *soul*, to what might seem more clearly apparent within cities, promising to come back later to consider its likeness in the soul, and whether those two forms of justice are really the same, or how they may be related. By the end of Book IX, however, when Socrates and his interlocutors have reached a glimpse 'in words' of the life truly devoted to wisdom and its contrast with the other, existing regimes, that initial analogy of the city and the soul, and the proper political activity of the philosopher, have become far more problematic:

As Glaucon objects at that point, the person who is wholeheartedly devoted to this regime of justice within himself 'won't be willing to mind the political things.'

'But yes,' Socrates replies, 'he will *in his own city*, very much so. However, perhaps he won't in his fatherland unless some divine chance coincidentally comes to pass.'

'I understand,' says Glaucon. 'You mean he will in the city whose foundation we have now gone through, the one that has its place in words (*logoi*), since I don't suppose it exists anywhere on earth.'

Then follows Socrates' response quoted above.

[12] The following summary very briefly paraphrases key points made in his *Taḥṣīl al-Saʿāda*, or *Attaining Happiness* (i.e., in the opening section of the trilogy probably intended by that name, where it is followed by accounts of the 'Philosophy of

readers into more serious engagement with and reflection on the deeper, perennial issues that are dealt with in his challenging and foundational works. Indeed if that was the case, he has certainly succeeded. For what other concern could be more practically central to each person's existence, so inescapable, and so rich and inexhaustible in its unavoidable—and recurrently problematic—connections to every area of our inner and outer life alike? Clearly, every aspect of that existential question is inseparable from our own starting point here in the process and the gradually unfolding demands of *taḥqīq*—of the ongoing tasks of 'verification' and 'realisation' necessarily embedded in the immediate, concrete context and real circumstances of each person's life. For if happiness still seems abstract and, for some, impossibly remote, then suffering, injustice, misery, despair and oppression certainly are not. As our earlier Qur'anic verse suggests, those '*places of darkening*' do ineluctably make each of us '*turn around*' and seek some way toward clarity, insight, illumination and direction.

At first each goal, each form of happiness, creates its own direction, its own distinctive orientation and path to travel. Thus we start with al-Fārābī because so many of the most powerful and accessible passages in his writing—indeed his most recurrent themes—focus on and take their bearings from that fundamental question of human ends. In many cases, he begins his discussion with an apparently simple enumeration of actual or potential ends or goals of human action. And as if to make those matters clearer, he often speaks (like Plato) of the ways those ends are *mirrored*—publicly, visibly, memorably, and also unavoidably—in the 'cities', in the various political, cultural and religious worlds we inhabit and continue to create together as human beings.[13]

Plato' and the 'Philosophy of Aristotle'). This distinctive allusion to 'happiness,' apparent in all of al-Fārābī's openly political writings, has deep philosophic roots in the issues and multiple perspectives of Aristotle's *Nichomachean Ethics* (which we know al-Fārābī commented on at length, although that commentary itself is now lost and known only from its citation in later authors); just as important are the intentional rhetorical echoes of its central symbolic usage in Qur'anic eschatology.

[13] 'Human beings (*insān*) are among those species which cannot complete those things which are necessary for them, nor attain the most excellent (*afḍal*) of their states, except through the association (*ijtimāʿ*) of many groups (*jamāʿāt*) of them in a single dwelling-place.' (*PR*, p. 69/*N*, p. 32).

But when al-Fārābī does speak of those distinctive human ends, he also always speaks of 'excellence', of their relative 'worth' or 'special distinction'.[14] For with the recognition of excellence comes the further question of superiority, relative value, purpose, and the possible connections between those ends—in short, of the hierarchy of human ends. And such a question, once again, is pre-eminently both theoretical and practical. Equally unavoidably, it is a question of intelligent choice, of the uniquely human freedom to choose on the basis of knowing the real hierarchy of ends.[15] And just as necessarily, that ongoing question of choice is always a subject of further reflection, discovery, criticism and deliberation, even before—but certainly always with—the further demands and limitations of realisation.

So with clarity of ends comes the further question of appropriate means—a question initially theoretical, perhaps, but even more unavoidably practical and political. To begin with, of course, it obliges us to inquire about what is given by 'nature', by the unavoidable circumstances and opportunities of this world in which we

---

References throughout this chapter to al-Fārābī's book sometimes known as '*al-Siyāsa al-Madanīya*' (see below on the significance of that particular title) are given first to the pages of the Arabic critical edition [*PR*] by Fauzi M. Najjar (Beirut, Imprimerie Catholique, 1964), then to the corresponding pages of the same author's partial English translation [*N*] ('The Political Regime'), pp. 31-57 in the volume *Medieval Political Philosophy: A Sourcebook*, ed. M. Mahdi and R. Lerner (Ithaca, Cornell University Press, 1972). For the purposes of this chapter, all our translations have been made independently, directly from the Arabic text, and therefore often differ from that previously published version; some more important differences are explained in footnotes below. See the Further Reading section below for a forthcoming new translation of this and other key political works by C. Butterworth.

[14] *Faḍl*: this term—which may best be rendered as 'excellence' in its Farabian context—is often translated in English and French as 'virtue'; for example, *al-madīna al-fāḍila* as 'the virtuous city'. But as al-Fārābī himself often emphatically points out, what are considered virtues, in most existing human associations, can typically mean very different things. The only true virtue he is concerned with in most contexts is that *distinctively human* (*insānī*) excellence (see preceding note) or perfection (*kamāl*), which is connected with the perfection of human intelligence (*ʿaql*), and which follows from (or necessarily contributes to) that uniquely human dimension of fulfilment.

[15] After describing the two sorts of animal-like 'desire' (*shawq*) and corresponding 'willing' (*irāda*) connected respectively with the appetitive and imaginative faculties of the soul, al-Fārābī then goes on to describe that unique third sort of

live.[16] But also, and usually far more problematically, it raises the challenging question of those *human 'natures'* with which we must work toward those ends, starting with our own. Which means discovering and learning to work with the actual and inescapable, dramatically differing innate capacities of each human being with regard to their intellectual, physical, verbal, creative and expressive, artistic, imaginative, moral, spiritual and many other skills and forms of reasoning and expression. (This is what al-Fārābī calls the spectrum of human 'natural' virtues.)

However, human beings are also quite visibly and unavoidably 'political' animals, and the general question of means for realising our ultimate ends and happiness is equally inseparable from all the interpenetrating forms and levels of our communal life and our culturally and historically determined, restricted and channelled expressions of those initially natural virtues. And those levels of realisation, he constantly reminds us,[17] extend seamlessly from one's initial, visible family and home, both spatially and temporally (and eventually even trans-spatially and trans-temporally), to the largest commonly visible communities of language and meaning, the civilisations brought into being over millennia by our prophets, poets and all the truly lasting 'legislators' both known and unknown. Within those particularly human political, cultural and social worlds, then,

---

willing which depends specifically on the rational part of the soul: 'At this point [after acquiring the basic rational principles], a third kind of will develops in the human being—the desire that is from understanding (*nuṭq*)—and this is what is specifically intended by the word "choice" (*ikhtiyār*). This is what comes to be uniquely and distinctively in the human being (*insān*), apart from the other animals. ...So when this (power of rational choice) has been realised in a human being, they are able to strive toward happiness, or not to strive for it, and with it the human being is able to do what is good and to do what is harmful and beautiful and ugly.' (*PR* 72/*N* 32-33)

[16] Including—al-Fārābī notably stresses (*N* 32-34)—the unique ways human beings are able to change and utilise even that naturally given world. There is a strikingly modern emphasis in al-Fārābī's repeated emphasis (here and in several other works) on changing and transforming the natural world, which certainly anticipates that peculiar focus on politically channelled technological possibilities and uses of science so prevalent only in the past two centuries of human history.

[17] The following points are only briefly alluded to (at *N* 38) in this text, but are dramatically and thoroughly illustrated throughout the remarkable 'historical' sections on the relations of philosophy and religions at the centre of al-Fārābī's extraordinary *Book of Letters* (*K. al-Ḥurūf*: see Further Reading below).

our initial, principial questions of possible ends and possible means always lead us on to other kinds of questions—and corresponding practical tasks.[18] What, in other words, are the practical and deliberative, moral and political 'virtues' needed to realise our highest human aims—what al-Fārābī, most disingenuously, loves to call our '*ultimate* happiness'? For the overall question of hierarchy and orientation, of the *actual practical interrelations* of all these factors, goals, givens and possibilities, seems to become almost impossibly complex at this point, at least if we remain in the realm of theory.

That is not all: this last immense set of questions surely raises yet another, even more troublesome possibility—and an equally unavoidable challenge. What are the *appropriate, effective means* needed to transform our existing possibilities (inner and outer) and our existing, so-called 'virtues' in the direction of what we eventually discover to be higher, more (or most) excellent ends? As we shall see, everything we have of al-Fārābī's writing suggests that, for him, philosophy is not so much a particular project as that wider, uniquely human task—inseparably both intellectual and practical—that is 'prospective' in its very essence. This aspect of his thought eventually leads us to the central practical human task of communication, or of 'instruction' and 'guidance', a further key dimension of his work that we will return to below—both in our discussion of al-Fārābī and in the following two chapters.

Finally, there is one critical dimension of al-Fārābī's philosophy of which he himself says very little, but which will emerge more explicitly in our discussion of the teachings of Ibn ʿArabī and Ostad Elahi below: the dimension of intention. Clarity about our ultimate ends, actual circumstances and available means—that is, a clear-sighted awareness of the true finality, the ultimate aim of all our actions—makes possible an extraordinary economy of effort and means, and a sometimes seemingly miraculous and enduring effectiveness, in any and every domain of life. Here, as in so many other ways, al-Fārābī's philosophical reflections, while not expressly 'spiritual' in their original formulation, carry over into every area of life.

[18] And without a constant awareness of the highest ends, al-Fārābī indicates, we are doomed to lose our truly human orientation, our 'true north'—just as it is largely through such repeated losses that we rediscover and gradually refine our awareness of those highest ends and our ultimate happiness.

CLARITY IN CONTEXT

None of the points just mentioned are—or indeed ever were—meant to be simply abstract philosophical questions. Ultimately, they are universal challenges every conscious person constantly faces in every conceivable earthly situation, whatever our particular age, culture, country, religion, century or social position. Al-Fārābī repeatedly points out that each of us is by necessity actually raising, resolving and responding to all these challenges—often, he suggests, in ways far more active, creative and resourceful than we might ever imagine—in the very process of life itself.[19] Within that wider, but always concrete and particular context, what philosophy—or at least al-Fārābī's own multi-faceted and often puzzling writings—can do, to begin with, is to help us to become more conscious, clear-sighted and eventually more insightful and creatively effective in actually responding to each of those challenges and the choices they reveal. For in any case, any answers his writings might suggest can only be tested and verified by the ongoing process of *taḥqīq* within our own lives and circumstances.[20]

The questions al-Fārābī raises might seem overwhelming at first, when one summarises them in their most general form, as we have just done here, in paraphrasing his magisterial *Attaining Happiness*. But their wider practical pertinence—indeed their unavoidability—becomes clear as soon as we raise them in any particular life-situation: as parents, as students searching for their vocation, young people choosing a life-partner, as colleagues (or managers and employees) in work or business, as advisors, creators, teachers, and so on. In all of those situations, our actual, practical choices and possibilities of realisation can often seem very limited at first sight. But one key implication of al-Fārābī's perspective is that ordinarily we have only to step back inwardly to a higher level of causality (final, formal or efficient, even where the 'material' factors may at first seem pre-determined) to discover many vitally important options and

[19] See the concluding words of his *Attaining Happiness* quoted at the end of this chapter.

[20] So any accounts of al-Fārābī's philosophy that suggest otherwise might best be taken as a mirror of their own author. See the relevant cautions in Further Reading below.

factors—and if nothing else, to clarify our own really *ultimate* intentions.[21] There is no question that al-Fārābī's thought, like Plato's, takes on its full poignancy and pertinence precisely in those recurrent life-situations of dis-orientation and destruction: that is, when we are consciously and unavoidably faced with rediscovering meaning after old certainties are lost; or with rebuilding our lives and reconstructing our human worlds in the aftermath of trauma, loss and apparent helplessness on any plane.[22]

Finally, simply raising all of these questions in any serious, conscious way obviously does involve considerable demands of inquiry (into the circumstances and possibilities actually present, as well as the relevant insights of others), reflection, and deliberation that would normally require much time, leisure and supportive company.[23] Yet ironically enough, al-Fārābī's decisive central questions seem to arise most pressingly and poignantly, in most people's lives, precisely in moments of crisis and uncertainty, when those supportive circumstances are rarely present. In any case, to say that al-Fārābī's philosophy is centrally and intrinsically 'political' should not raise anything like the familiar contemporary media images of parties, activists, politicians and the like. The perspectives he raises—and his lasting historical influences—are clearly more far-reaching than that.

[21] There is a very effective and revealing practical spiritual exercise—although the process is also amply illustrated by any number of powerful literary and cinematic examples—which anyone can undertake to illuminate this point. (However, the exercise works most effectively with another person present to pose the questions.) It consists in being repeatedly asked the question 'what would you do if you knew that you had only x-amount of time left to live?', while the questioner gradually shortens the imagined life-span in question from the decades we usually imagine down to a matter of years, months, weeks, then days and minutes. Not surprisingly, the deepest revelations usually come only when one has reached the very shortest, most immediate intervals.

[22] That is, in the defining human situation of *khusr* (loss, calamity, insoluble dilemma, despair, etc.) so beautifully expressed in the particular Sura (*al-ʿAṣr*, 103) which opens this book.

[23] Again, note the pointed Qur'anic stress in our thematic Sura (103, in the Preface and Introduction above) on our 'mutual counselling and support' (*tawāṣin*) in realizing 'what is Real/Right', and on our 'spiritual perseverance' (*ṣabr*) as the key practical, active conditions for moving beyond that initial state of loss to full humanity.

POSSIBLE COMMUNITIES AND THE HIERARCHY OF ENDS

Throughout history, it seems that al-Fārābī's book often called *al-Siyāsa al-Madanīya* (translated as 'The Political Regime') has remained the best known and most accessible of his writings. Interestingly enough, any attempt to translate the key term *al-siyāsa* in its title actually helps to highlight the manifold intentions and much wider potential applications of his work. To begin with, al-Fārābī's *siyāsa* is not a noun: he is not simply talking abstractly about some broad 'theory' of reified political structures existing independently of our own participation and responsibility. Instead, his particular emphasis in using the distinctive Arabic 'verbal-noun' (*masḍar*) form pointedly serves to highlight the active, individually participatory and responsible engagement of each reader in the realities al-Fārābī has in mind.[24] In other words, his book is about our actually organising, ordering, 'structuring-and-managing', directing, guiding and leading any particular human association, as well as the abstract or institutional forms of management, organisation and structure which may flow from that creative activity.[25] Once we have sketched out al-Fārābī's basic discussion of the hierarchy of human ends and forms of communication, we will move on to illustrate the immediate applicability of his ideas in all the relevant spheres of our actual life: family, school, work, and so on.

[24] This same point applies equally to the title of al-Fārābī's other major programmatic work with which we began this essay, his *Taḥṣīl al-Saᶜāda*, which we have consistently translated here as '*Attaining* Happiness'—i.e., the lifelong, real process by which people actually go about realising and achieving both the various human-animal and ultimate human forms of happiness. (*Taḥṣīl* has the same grammatical structure and similar complexities to the key term *taḥqīq* discussed in our Introduction above.) With any of these key Arabic terms, the immediately active verbal, participatory emphasis of the *maṣdar* is lost whenever it is translated as a noun, a sort of reified abstraction or concept, in English and other Indo-European languages. (The resulting fundamental loss, incidentally, is vastly more far-reaching in all existing English translations of the Qur'an.)

[25] All of these expressions capture different practical facets of the integrative, orientative task of *siyāsa*. Thus readers today may well find that the central human issues and practical tasks al-Fārābī examines in this work are far more actively, thoughtfully, vividly and creatively tackled in works to be found in bookstore sections dealing with 'management' or 'personal growth/fulfilment' and the like, than in the academic literatures of what is today called 'political science' or 'philosophy'.

Thus the fact that al-Fārābī begins his political account of our human situation by identifying the fundamental roots of the possible forms and aims of human association in a careful summary of Aristotelian epistemology and psychology[26] only highlights his insistence that the fields of application of this quintessentially human task of *siyāsa* always remain grounded in human souls and our spectrum of forms of knowing, in all their full diversity and potentiality. This task of comprehensive ordering and guidance (*siyāsa*) necessarily begins with those souls—thus above all with the orientation and direction of one's *own* self—and inevitably extends from there through all conceivable forms of association and organisation. So as we have already emphasised, the full relevance and power of al-Fārābī's perspectives can only be grasped when we first apply them to contexts and situations which we already know intimately. Those are the 'associations' existentially bound up with our own relevant individual fields of choice and desire, of intentionality and happiness: workplace, family, school, friends, the ambient media, and all those other immediate forms of association in which we actually play an active and (at least potentially) responsible role.[27]

Al-Fārābī himself strongly suggests (and it is easy enough to verify in any case) that the fundamental philosophic considerations he raises—of our ultimate ends, means, and the choices and skills

[26] Although readers are by no means obligated to accept the particular psychology and epistemology outlined here and in his many other commentaries on Aristotle's works, or in his later philosophical interpreters. In fact, professional students of al-Fārābī's writings will quickly recognise that I do not find those particular ancient epistemological theories (nor their ontological assumptions, one might add) either adequately comprehensive or phenomenologically convincing—and that our discussion here does not at all assume that the coherence and ongoing philosophic relevance of al-Fārābī's writing depends on his readers accepting *en bloc* such classical Aristotelian views, even if they were originally assumed by al-Fārābī himself.

[27] That is, these relevant spheres are unlikely today to be in domains popularly termed as 'politics' or 'religion', unless one happens to be a professional working in what one's ambient culture describes in such terms—or else the citizen of one of the many new nation-states recently and ostentatiously constructed around some particular ethno-religious ideology. But even in those particular exceptional cases, the terms 'politics' and 'religion', in contemporary usage (anywhere in the world) are normally far too narrowly and specifically construed to recall the deeper realities and tasks al-Fārābī actually intends.

required to transform or realise the expression of those factors—necessarily apply 'homologously', in structurally analogous ways, across the full range of human associations. On the other hand, if we take the philosophical touchstones he provides us only separately and in the abstract, applying them to unfamiliar situations and distant historical contexts far removed from our own concrete domains of actual choice and responsibility—such as 'politics' and 'religion' as they are usually presented in mass media—then al-Fārābī's ideas, like the views of some of Plato's more dramatic personae, will almost inevitably strike his readers initially as primarily critical and even provocative, before we can begin to grasp their more constructive and deeply liberating implications.

Thus al-Fārābī begins the philosophic core of his book[28] with a broad account of the spectrum of human ends and potential choices, followed by a much more pointedly detailed reminder of the radically differing natural human capacities both to *perceive* and then to *actualise* or realise those ends and corresponding forms of real and of imagined or partial happiness. Only then does he turn to the corresponding forms of cities and human associations more generally.[29]

[28] Of course this overtly political section begins quite unexpectedly, roughly *halfway* through his book (*PR* 69), preceded by 31 Arabic pages of a detailed 'cosmology' or ontology—which careful readers of his subsequent account of the 'beliefs' of the truly noble city here (or students of certain of his other key works, especially the *Attaining Happiness*) will immediately recognise as a detailed 'political theology'. (These long opening sections help explain why the same book has also been transmitted historically under the alternative descriptive title 'The First Principles of the Beings'.) Some helpful introductions to the characteristic esoteric rhetorical structures and intentions of al-Fārābī's writings, revolving around his conceptions of philosophy and religions, are indicated in our section on Further Reading below.

[29] Al-Fārābī pointedly reminds his reader at each stage of this typology that his distinctions cover *all* corresponding human 'associations' (*ijtimāʿ*). The Arabic adjective al-Fārābī uses to describe this full spectrum of all potential human groups and associations, *madanīya*, comes explicitly from the same historical reference-point as the English term 'political': i.e., the *polis*, or *madīna*, considered as the smallest possible human association needed for actually realising the *highest* human ends. The following summaries and short quotations are taken from *PR*, pages 79-107 (= *N*, pages 36-56, with some important omissions), which includes a great deal of material openly adapted from Plato's *Republic* or later summaries thereof. As can be seen from the notes required here to explain, illuminate and qualify many of al-Fārābī's key terms, the existing English translation (*N*) offers

The typology he develops there, starting out with a fairly detailed description of the structures and requisite features of the ideal 'virtuous', 'good' and 'truly happy' city,[30] is based, to begin with, on the corresponding ends of each type of association. Hence the defining aim of the truly excellent city, the 'true and supreme happiness', is said to consist in *knowing*—which was earlier shown to be the distinctive perfection of the truly human soul—to the degree possible for each of its inhabitants.

As if to highlight the centrality of knowing as the essentially human (*insānī*) goal of our existence and of the truly human forms of association, al-Fārābī begins his account of all the other forms of association—which, by the terms of his preceding description of the truly virtuous city, would clearly include virtually all historically known human associations—by calling their residents as a whole 'the people of (the period of) ignorance'.[31] That is, those cities and other associations are, by definition, based on ignorance of our highest human ends, in that they are oriented primarily toward one or another of those multitude of possible goals which people share with other animals, rather than the ultimate human perfection of true knowing. Unlike his long and complex description of the 'city of (true) excellence' as thoroughly oriented toward knowing in all its

---

severe obstacles to readers who cannot refer directly to the underlying Arabic; hopefully these will be remedied in the complete forthcoming translation (see Further Reading below).

[30] And more importantly, of the rare 'virtuous (excellent) human beings', the accomplished philosophers who are 'strangers' in all the other existing cities, but the seeds and potential founders of any wider, fully human community (*PR* 80/*N* 37). Used in an explicitly Islamic context, al-Fārābī's mention of the term 'stranger' (*gharīb*) could not but evoke recollections of—and deeper reflection upon—the famous hadith: *Islam began as a stranger and will again return, as it began, as a stranger. So blessed are those who are strangers!.*

[31] *Ahl al-jāhilīya, PR* 87. For any Arabic and predominantly Muslim readership, al-Fārābī's rhetoric here is clearly intended to evoke an immediate association with the familiar classical (originally Qur'anic) contrast between the brutal period of Arabian ethical and cultural chaos and barbarity preceding the Qur'anic revelation (*al-jāhilīya*), and the new ethico-political order instituted by the Prophet and his earliest supporters. Throughout his ensuing discussion of the different imperfect associations, al-Fārābī continues to refer to the practices, customs and cultures of this undefined *ahl al-jāhilīya* in ways which would clearly continue to suggest, to less critical or reflective readers, that he is somehow referring (exclusively) to various pre-Islamic cultures, Persian and Hellenistic Greek as well as Arab.

levels and forms, al-Fārābī here intentionally describes each of these forms of association only very briefly, in their most abstract, schematic terms, focusing only on the particular predominant goal or purpose underlying and 'orienting' the specific association in question. He does not give examples—although even his most uneducated reader could (and should) provide vivid contemporary illustrations of most of the types he mentions—as almost any specific historical illustration might well keep his intended readers from grasping the ongoing, intended relevance of his typology as a touchstone for their own existence and their own corresponding tasks of orientation and realisation.

As al-Fārābī goes on to enumerate them, this vast spectrum of possible social groupings begins with the '*necessary* association',[32] those based on co-operation in procuring what is needed for basic survival and subsistence. This is followed by the '*vile* city'[33] that is directed solely toward acquiring wealth and avoiding expenditure, the 'associations of vile citizens'. Next comes the '*base* city',[34] whose citizens co-operate in the pursuit of sensual or imaginary pleasures and play. His descriptions of each group or association up to this point are exceedingly brief, while his discussions of the internal structures,

[32] Translated in N as the '*indispensable*' association, also the familiar starting point in Plato's *Republic*.

[33] The unusual Arabic qualifier here (*ridhāla*) could just as easily be translated as 'base', 'contemptible' or 'despicable', although clearly al-Fārābī's intention does not reflect any particular moral opprobrium attached to wealth as such, but rather the fact that the characteristic citizens of this association are, by definition, entirely *unaware* of any other potential human ends. As such, this association is virtually a subset of the preceding one devoted only to life's necessities. al-Fārābī goes on to highlight in some detail the central, but differently functioning, roles of *wealth* in the life of each of the following imperfect regimes, particularly in the 'timocratic' and the 'all-inclusive' ('democratic') types of association.

[34] The Arabic terms used here (*khissa*, *khasīs*, at *PR* 89) are very close in meaning to those describing the preceding association (*ridhāla*, preceding note), and only the actual description of its ends really brings out the distinctive differences of aims. It may not be accidental that the adjective al-Fārābī uses to qualify this particular sort of association differs by only one small dot from the Arabic root for the '*senses*' (*ḥiss*), providing a striking sort of visual pun—a rhetorical procedure frequently employed in all literatures using the Arabic alphabet—pointedly reminding readers of his preceding explanation of the way each of these types of association is ultimately rooted in corresponding dimensions and possibilities of human psychology.

dynamics and rulership/management of the following three types are far more lengthy and subtle, no doubt suggesting ways in which those next three associations might potentially be transformed in the direction of actually realising the highest human ends.

Thus the 'city of *nobility*'[35] and all the associations based on common notions of honour and nobility are those whose citizens are united in the pursuit of any of those many forms of 'honour' and 'merit' which are not defined by the actual human perfection of knowing: that is, which are instead based on the acquisition of necessities, wealth, means of pleasure, fame, or power and domination —all the defining characteristics of each of the other 'ignorant' associations. At the very end of his long discussion of this type of association (*PR* 93-94), al-Fārābī stresses that 'this city resembles the truly virtuous city because of [its hierarchical recognition of different forms of excellence]', and even adds that 'this city is the *best* of the cities of the people of ignorance.'

Al-Fārābī then moves on to explain that the 'city of domination'[36] is any association whose ruling part (be it an individual, group or the entire city) is uniquely oriented toward domination

[35] The abstract Arabic form employed here, *karāma*, would immediately recall, for al-Fārābī's original readers, their conceptions of the person who is *karīm*—perhaps closest in meaning to the English (and underlying Greek) notions of 'magnanimity' and 'generosity of soul'. This was one of the central moral ideals of pre-Islamic Arabic society, and—if one can judge, for example, by slightly later depictions in Firdawsī's *Shāhnāmeh*—probably likewise conveyed at least some of the idealised, chivalric ideals of pre-Islamic Sassanid, Persian civilisation shared by some of al-Fārābī's contemporary cosmopolitan readers. (In particular, al-Fārābī and his readers were certainly aware of later Sassanid kings' patronage or protection of philosophy and other forms of Hellenistic science that had been severely persecuted and almost eliminated by the particular Christian forms of rulership instituted by successive Byzantine emperors.)

[36] The actual Arabic terminology used here (*taghallub, ghalaba*, etc.: *PR* 94-99) is highly *descriptive* of the different processes, forms and aims of 'domination' involved in rulership (*riyāsa*)—including, one suspects, even the 'supreme rulership' of the 'virtuous' city (and most certainly of each of the other associations). At the same time, it is entirely lacking in the specific historical connotations and often highly individual focus inherent in English terms like 'despot' or 'tyrant' ('tyranny', etc.) unfortunately used in the existing English translation. This is one of many places where al-Fārābī clearly goes beyond his possible earlier Hellenistic sources in creative ways which are not adequately conveyed in existing translations and many published historical accounts of his thought and writing.

of others *as an end in itself*, not simply in order to achieve any of the other 'ignorant' ends already mentioned. But his lengthy explanation there of the many processes and forms of domination involved in rulership and governance may involve more generally applicable lessons as well.

Finally, he concludes with a description of the 'all-inclusive' or 'comprehensive' city,[37] in terms which strongly evoke what historians have depicted of Baghdad and the other great cosmopolitan Muslim trading metropolises in al-Fārābī's own Abbasid era, not to mention their more numerous world-wide equivalents in the modern age. This is the city, he points out, which encompasses 'all kinds of desires and ways of life', including all the ends of the other ignorant cities, 'in a most perfect manner'. Thus it is also likely to include, after some time, some of those noble human beings and philosophers, the real 'knowers', who are the only possible founders of any truly human and virtuous/excellent association. That is why he can say, in conclusion, that this association 'possesses both good and evil to a greater degree than the rest of the cities of the age of ignorance'.

As a second key typological analysis—which he gradually unfolds *within* his discussion of each of these preceding types of association, both truly human and ignorant—, al-Fārābī devotes special attention to the 'internal' forms of order and corresponding *motivations* which must be carefully manipulated and consciously established in order to maintain—or to found and create—each particular type of human association. In other words, he focuses his reader's attention

[37] The purely descriptive term al-Fārābī actually uses here at *PR* 99-101 (*jamāᶜīya*, from the same root as his 'association', *ijtimāᶜ*) is entirely devoid of all the multitude of original Greek connotations of 'democracy' as having to do with an unruly and dangerous, inherently fickle *demos*, always tempted by tyranny or despotism and the like, which are still deeply embedded in the modern European-language equivalents of that Greek term. Al-Fārābī's focus here is much more clearly on the *multiplicity* and *diversity* of human ends pursued by various participants in such associations—potentially including even the highest human ends of real knowing— and not on any particular element of that wider mixture. In particular, his analysis of rulership in such associations, with its typical dependence on the distribution of wealth and munificence, is not only marvellously descriptive of most existing democracies today. It may also much better convey the actual dynamics of power, wealth and authority in his own Abbasid Baghdad than the arbitrary autocratic fantasies of the '*Arabian Nights*' and later romanticized images of the glories of al-Fārābī's own era.

on the internal dynamics and essential complex mechanisms of guidance, direction and control—and on the alternative processes of disorder, disintegration and eventual transformation—which are practically demanded by each of those particular guiding ends. He begins his analysis of authority in each case by outlining the most obvious political instruments of (a) incentives and disincentives (i.e. bribes and threats), whose particular forms necessarily vary according to the dominant ends in each particular type of organisation. In addition, as we have already noted, he carefully points out (b) a number of recurrent situations normally requiring outright force and physical domination.[38]

Throughout this discussion, in keeping with his wider emphasis in his numerous other writings on the essential political roles of religions, al-Fārābī pays particular attention in each case to (c) the more subtle and pervasive role of established opinions and habitual or customary belief-systems in establishing and maintaining any of these actually existing imperfect forms of human association. This practically fundamental political role of what we could broadly call the establishment and manipulation of deeper cultural factors of popular belief and custom (or in al-Fārābī's context, and still in some recent nation-states, of more visibly 'religious' elements of persuasion and social conditioning) is certainly inseparable from the central role of rhetoric—understood in this broad and centrally political sense—which is highlighted in so many of al-Fārābī's other specialised writings, especially his famous commentaries on the Aristotelian canon of logic and demonstration.[39]

Al-Fārābī concludes his enumeration of these possible forms of human association, and his entire book on the *Political Regimes*, with two additional, curiously suggestive, brief discussions. First, he draws his readers' attention to the existence of two other distinctive

[38] In particular, he bluntly recognises their indispensable roles both in safely pacifying criminal or otherwise deficient natures, and in making possible the very establishment of each of the non-despotic regimes. One might add that, unlike Plato, he says very little here about the unavoidable defensive roles of *warfare* for every broader 'political regime': this particular (relative) omission may have implications for grasping what he actually intends by his constant focus in this particular work on his ideal, 'virtuous city'. (See the concluding section on Communication and Community at the end of this chapter.)

[39] See Further Reading below.

variant forms of each of the ignorant cities or associations. These are the corresponding classes of (a) the 'sinning' cities, which were once—so he says[40]—actually virtuous, but now retain only the 'opinions' of the virtuous city, while actually pursuing the ends and actions of the ignorant cities. Then, he continues, there is also the corresponding class of (b) the different 'erring' cities,[41] which are likewise in actuality no different from the other ignorant cities (in terms of the ends and actions they actually pursue), but whose citizens again believe in and follow opinions which are outwardly different from those of the explicitly, self-consciously 'ignorant' regimes—and perhaps thereby more amenable to reform or to 'rehabilitation' in a more excellent or virtuous direction.

Finally, at the very end of his book, he concludes with a strange discussion of those specific rare human individuals whom he calls the 'weeds' in the virtuous city. These individuals are those potential philosophers, with all the extremely rare natural aptitudes for true knowing and perfection of that essential human capacity, who have failed to complete their philosophical task and have instead become mere sophists, rhetoricians, ideologists and the like. That is, they are either useless in communicating and establishing true knowing (and all its accompanying virtues) in others; or they have refused that essential responsibility and found their knowing useful only for

[40] His intentionally creative usage of this particular 'mytho-history' is amply illustrated in his *K. al-Ḥurūf* (see n. 17 above); see also the further discussion of that key text in M. Mahdi's foundational studies discussed in Further Reading below.

[41] The adjectives he uses here (*PR* 103-104) to describe these two broad sorts of 'ignorant' associations (*fāsiqa* and *ḍālla*) are both explicitly drawn from the Qur'an. As such, they are clearly intended to suggest two recurrent Qur'anic categories, for both individuals and earlier human communities: (1) those who knowingly 'sin' or infringe what they do already accept to be the proper moral or religious norms, which they simply fail to carry out appropriately in actual practice; and (2) those whose intentions are good, but who are unconsciously 'wandering astray' or 'lost' because they simply do not know any better. In drawing these distinctions—and so openly highlighting their Qur'anic correspondences for his Muslim readers—al-Fārābī is also pointedly suggesting the appropriate approaches of action and communication needed for reforming or transforming 'associations' (or individuals) of either type. Since few of his readers are likely to have mistaken their own surroundings for the perfect, 'excellent city'—while many of them, as we know, were vigorously seeking alternative possibilities of reform—these final remarks would have constituted particularly pointed practical suggestions.

themselves and associates who would pursue with them the lower, ignorant (infra-human) ends. In either case, they have failed to fulfil the tasks of their further perfection because they lacked some of the essential natural or moral or deliberative qualifications and virtues required to motivate and enable them to go out and communicate and actualise their wisdom in others.[42]

Now both of these concluding discussions highlight wider themes that pervade and indeed help to explain the very existence of all of al-Fārābī's other works. Those are first, his clear-sighted recognition of the human necessity and the actual possibilities of reform (or of even more fundamental transformation disguised as reform) of existing associations and situations in the direction of realising the highest human ends. And secondly, the discovery and actualisation of the corresponding moral, political and natural qualities of leadership, dedication and philanthropic virtues and skills which are all necessary in order to transform an intellectually apt, 'philo-sophical' individual into a genuinely effective, positive and lastingly influential force within their wider community. In both of these areas, it appears al-Fārābī is quite realistically suggesting here that it is typically far easier to begin to transform an existing situation toward the actual realisation of higher ends by presenting one's creative project as a 'reform' or 'return' to already commonly acknowledged ends and ideals (or as the completion and perfection of an already existing accomplishment),[43] rather than having to motivate and unify large numbers of suitably qualified people around an entirely new project of realisation.

[42] This somewhat enigmatic passage at the end of the *PR* is beautifully illuminated and complemented by the longer corresponding concluding section of al-Fārābī's *Attaining Happiness* (i.e. the end of the first part of that trilogy, which is also edited and widely known under the same name as the trilogy itself). That more detailed, philosophically fascinating work also makes it much clearer why the truly 'complete' human being requires, not only special intellectual abilities, but also all of these different natural, moral and deliberative forms of excellence in order to bring wisdom into being, in the appropriate and possible ways, in a wider community.

[43] This is most obviously the approach, of course, followed by so many famous movements and figures of renewal (most notably through the notion of the religious 'renewer', the *mujaddid*) throughout Islamic history.

APPLYING AL-FARABI'S INSIGHTS: CLARITY AND TRANSFORMATION

To recapitulate what we have just seen in detail, the ongoing interest of al-Fārābī's writing is in its rigorous demands of orientation: in the way it forces us first to consider carefully the existence of higher, alternative human ends (whatever the particular associations in which we are necessarily involved); and then to discover the corresponding responsibility and concrete demands of communication and transformation needed to make those highest ends real. Now with that broad goal in mind, this initial summary outline of al-Fārābī's discussion of human ends and associations can only exaggerate (as with Plato) several obvious and recurrent dangers for anyone approaching his writings for the first time.

To start with, it is easy enough for the uninitiated reader to imagine that al-Fārābī here is simply outlining some sort of familiar, superficial abstract schema or typology of 'political science'. But even if that reader makes the additional effort to apply al-Fārābī's touchstones to their own operative associations and life-circumstances, it is all too easy at first to focus on the 'debunking', obviously critical and often painfully revealing results of his initial awakening of our awareness of alternative ends. It is also rather easy, and certainly more dangerous, for a more probing and cynical reader to leave aside al-Fārābī's talk of higher ends and instead focus simply on his morally unclouded lessons about the actual dynamics of manipulation and control in any particular associative or political context. Years of teaching al-Fārābī's thought to young students would suggest that Plato's memorable dramatisations of each of those possible pitfalls, in so many of his dialogues, are only too deeply rooted in constant realities of human nature, unless the energy, intellectual acuity and critical aptitudes of youth are profoundly tempered and informed by the educational experiences and deeper challenges of actual wider responsibility. Fortunately al-Fārābī, like Plato, becomes ever more fascinating and revealing with age. Even a quick historical glance at the most creative and lastingly influential direct interpreters of his work—figures such as Avicenna, Ibn Khaldūn, Averroes,

Maimonides, Naṣīr al-Dīn al-Ṭūsī and the like—beautifully illustrates how constructive and remarkably far-reaching the deeper appropriation of his intentions can be.[44]

In short, al-Fārābī's constantly clear-sighted focus on the potential ends and actual dynamics of any given human context—which always has to begin with each reader's own unique life-situation—can be fruitful and constructively revealing precisely to the degree that we apply it in the spirit of that famous prayer which opened this chapter. That is, his teaching comes to life when we are able to use his keys to concentrate clearly, without any illusion or self-delusion, on the realities of what is given in our actual situation, including the real possibilities—and all the corresponding limits—of transformation to a higher, genuinely effective human end. One does not have to look far afield to find the domains in which those keys are applicable: every human institution, by the time it has even become recognisable as an 'institution', is already well on the way to its inevitably self-serving, self-preoccupied end of decay, disillusionment and dissolution, unless it is constantly renewed, transformed and recreated as an effective instrument for actually realising the highest, fully human ends, beyond its own survival. Those processes and creative possibilities are normally most obvious—and certainly most easily remedied—precisely in the 'human ecology' or 'micro-cosmos' of our individual lives and familiar local contexts: within our families, schools, local religious groupings (mosque, church, *ṭarīqa*, etc.), businesses and enterprises, medical and other 'social services', and the like. The concluding Postscript of this book provides several suggestive illustrations of that basic Farabian principle.

Much of al-Fārābī's own writing—and certainly most of what is apparently original in it and creatively adapted to his own historical challenges—had to do precisely with suggesting creative ways of adapting to and transforming the new historical circumstances brought about by the cultural and political domination, in his own day, of 'opinions' and related 'virtues' expressed in the languages of the then relatively new religions broadly associated with Islam

[44] See some helpful references to important illustrative studies of those still influential classical interpreters in Further Reading below.

and Christianity. But we have already tried to suggest above—and again in our Postscript below—the many ways in which it would be dangerous and misleading to continue to focus on broadly reified generalities about any 'religion' or 'politics'. For we live today in a world in which the operative forms of human association, culture and *siyāsa* are increasingly global, implicit (pervasively unconscious), and often no longer outwardly or primarily expressed in terms of what contemporary cultures tend to view as either 'religion' or 'politics'. Even in those unfortunate situations where the functional presence of what people today have come to call religion and politics has been almost exclusively reduced to mass ideologies—or in al-Fārābī's terms, to the openly manipulative use of popularly accepted opinions and symbols purely for limited purposes of momentary political manipulation—he would suggest that we still have to start by clearly observing and consciously recognising those underlying realities as they actually lie before us. Only then can we have any realistic hope either of constructively 'using' such ideologies (a dangerously problematic temptation!), or of otherwise cooperating creatively to transform our concretely existing situations in the direction of actually realising higher human ends.

DIMENSIONS OF COMMUNICATION

It is surely not coincidental that the philosophers of the Islamic world have for centuries continued to acknowledge al-Fārābī, after Aristotle, as the 'Second Teacher'. For the larger issues and means of communication, of rhetoric, education and realisation, are central in all of his surviving work, especially when it came to applying the insights and intentions of philosophy in new situations where the ongoing political issues we have just mentioned were now largely expressed in ostensibly religious terms and institutions.[45] Indeed if

[45] A particularly dramatic and—like Plato's stay in Syracuse, hopefully edifying—very recent example of such an attempted 'application' of philosophically inspired teachings directly in the political realm is the case of Ayatollah Khomeini and many of the other philosophically educated clerics active in the latest Iranian revolution, many of whose distinctive institutions were explicitly adopted from traditions of Islamic philosophy still profoundly rooted in al-Fārābī's political teachings, and even in Plato's *Republic.*

many of the world's dominant 'associations' had remained ostensibly and publicly Marxist, as was the case only a few decades ago, then al-Fārābī's contemporary relevance would have been even more obvious. Perhaps because the origins of that particular ideology and the real underpinnings of Marxism's historical establishment are still so relatively transparent, the immediate relevance of al-Fārābī's categories and understanding of the particular 'prophets' and 'successors', 'revealed books' and 'political hermeneutics' involved could not have escaped any serious reader in such regimes.[46] But when we move beyond—or more deeply beneath—those unfortunate polities where such ideologies are still locally dominant and inescapable, what does al-Fārābī still have to teach us today?

Perhaps the most obvious domain lies in the immense area of 'communication', which is—as al-Fārābī so clearly and persuasively demonstrates—the essential groundwork and accompaniment of any effective process of transformation. In that regard, we may recall one essential point already developed in the earlier summary of his typology of different human associations in terms of their particular ends and their internal dynamics of control and perpetuation. Just as there is a natural hierarchy of human ends, there is also a corresponding natural hierarchy of forms of communication. First (and indispensably), there is the task of awakening of each person's awareness of the highest human ends—of our knowing or awareness of *things as they really are*—to the degree that is possible in each case. Secondly, there are all the corresponding forms of persuasion and symbolic 'imitation' (to use al-Fārābī's term) or foreshadowing of that actual awareness, but without its complete realisation as actual knowing. In this shifting shadow-domain of politically effective beliefs and opinions, al-Fārābī constantly reiterates that there are many relative degrees of symbolic imitation and apprehension of the highest truths, and correspondingly immense possibilities of

[46] Here I cannot help but recall the striking experience in Tehran, several decades ago, of studying al-Fārābī's political philosophy—as expressed in the influential Avicennan commentaries of Naṣīr al-Dīn al-Ṭūsī (and the theological critiques of Fakhr Rāzī)—together with a cohort of still devoutly pious Maoist Chinese exchange students, all of whom managed to remain blithely unaware of the dramatic relevance of each line of Ṭūsī's understanding of prophecy and subsequent authority and interpretation to their own personal and public situation!

purifying and perfecting those symbols and their forms of teaching in the direction of more complete and adequate understanding. Thirdly, and no doubt most commonly and universally, he is quite explicit about all the infinitely variegated forms of manipulation relying on human beings' 'animal' desires and fears, and on each ruler's corresponding imaginal and real incitement of those desires. (Most obviously, in the increasingly global consumer culture, this concern of al-Fārābī is wonderfully reflected in all the ever-changing forms and expressions of what we call advertising and publicity.) And finally, there is the irreducible base level of physical force and domination, in all its public and more private expressions.

If any reader still requires a particular context for more concrete illustrations of each of these key points, we need only think—for all four of these indispensable levels of communication—of the actual structures of public 'educational' systems anywhere in the contemporary world. Or even more vividly, no doubt the actual internal functioning of different families well illustrates the same broad spectrum of possible forms and degrees of communication—and suggests how profoundly and intimately al-Fārābī's 'political' philosophy engages our common human condition. The ultimate spiritual laws, he suggests, like the crucibles in which we are each obliged to discover and realise them, are anything but esoteric.

Now the eschatological 'secret' of al-Fārābī's thought—no less than with Ibn ʿArabī and Ostad Elahi in the following chapters—is simple to express in words. No actual transformation of the human condition—or to use the Qur'anic language which frames this book, no movement from the common human-animal (*bashar*) to a genuinely theomorphic and actualised human being (*insān*)—can ever begin without this first and highest form of communication: the fundamental task of awakening the awareness of our higher human ends. To take the more visible examples of our public associations, it quickly becomes obvious that every one of al-Fārābī's 'ignorant', 'immoral' or 'erring' polities, without any exception, involves an unavoidable ongoing process of multi-faceted conflict and warfare, only more or less covert or publicly visible. This inherent conflict, he makes clear, is twofold: over the acquisition and distribution of the particular 'goods' in question (health and survival, wealth, pleasures, honours, domination, etc.), where some temporary, conventional agreement exists about a particular widely accepted set of goods; and also, on top of that, between those various material and socially established 'goods', whenever that temporary consensus of ends begins to break down—as it necessarily always will, whether the precipitating cause be internal or external shocks and challenges.

In other words, to make very explicit what al-Fārābī leaves for each of his readers to discover: the only real (as opposed to visibly existing) hierarchy of human ends, the only truly human community of ends, is what he calls the 'virtuous' or 'excellent city', however and in whatever context that reality may come to exist. So to return to our starting point and the fundamental question of orientation, the most lastingly effective way people can come to recognize that one fully human (*insānī*) community is through their ongoing 'educational experience' of its infinitely varied contraries, which new human souls continue to have to discover for themselves—at every level and in every domain of our lives—in this carefully designed crucible.[47]

In radical contrast to this ongoing, visible political condition of disequilibrium and unavoidable conflict, the highest human ends of knowing and awareness—however they may be understood and actualised—immediately stand out as being intrinsically 'immaterial' and therefore potentially achievable by each person, without having to take anything away from any other.[48] More than that, by their very nature the achievement of those highest ends both requires and spontaneously creates mutually beneficial and intrinsically co-operative communities oriented toward the actualisation of those distinctively human ends.

When we look at the history of religions, in particular, what we always discover—whatever the particular religion or historical

[47] See the further allusions to this central Qur'anic eschatological symbolism—of the essential purifying, educational role of the 'Fire' and 'Gehenna'—throughout each of the following essays, and in our studies of Ibn ʿArabī's eschatology cited in Further Reading below.

[48] In modern terms, we could say that the 'politics of realisation' or of human transformation—unlike the inherent political dynamics of each of al-Fārābī's imperfect 'ignorant' or 'erring' cities, is uniquely *not* a 'zero-sum game'—indeed something like its absolute contrary!

situation involved—is that genuinely spiritual communities always come into being almost invisibly and spontaneously, around a particular human being, or tiny group of spiritual companions, who have actually realised and expressed those highest human ends. And often those small communities just as mysteriously disintegrate and disappear with the passing of the actualised presence of that 'Friend of God'.[49] So-called 'religious institutions', as we all eventually learn in life, are a radically different sort of thing, and the not infrequent confusion of common names and appellations cannot obscure the radically different realities in question in either case.

Therefore while everyone lives, at different times and in different contexts, in situations which both subject us to and require of us the more or less skilful use of persuasion, manipulation and force, al-Fārābī constantly reminds us that the highest, indispensable human task is to awaken ourselves and others to those highest human ends of knowing and awareness. Once we have recognised that, the other practical consequences gradually become clear and naturally fall into place. Most obviously and immediately, the intrinsically valuable, uniquely human satisfactions and entirely disproportionate rewards which come from that awakening of one's own and other souls are so powerful and radically different from the other 'human-animal' ends al-Fārābī has mentioned that it is doubtful whether many people who have seriously tasted that actualised knowing would ever be willing to spend their lives in any other pursuit. For example, my often very clever and ambitious young students in philosophy and religion frequently raise the very practical question why apparently intelligent, privileged and highly capable people will so often devote their adult lives to such unpaid or outwardly demanding and—materially speaking—poorly 'rewarded' occupations as raising children, nursing, teaching (at any level), working in childcare, social services and the like? Or why such gifted individuals often so avidly pursue the onerous lifelong disciplines of artistic and creative activities (poetry,

[49] In Islamic terms, the Qur'anic *walī Allāh* (or in Persian poetry, the beloved Friend, the *dûst* and *yâr*), the fully realized soul who is truly 'near' to and protected by that Source.

theatre, music, writing, painting, and the like) where their rational chances of any visible rewards of money, fame or power are equally close to non-existent? What we have already mentioned of al-Fārābī's thought should suggest the obvious—if not always initially agreeable—answer to their repeated interrogation.

On another level, but no less practically, what al-Fārābī mentions about the hierarchy of human ends and forms of communication should make each of us extremely sensitive to any claims (or temptations, where one's self is concerned) to be employing persuasion, manipulation or force in the ostensible service of the highest, uniquely human ends. This is not to suggest that such efforts are not ultimately necessary, and in many cases even unavoidable. But the actually lasting (indeed only lasting) 'power' and 'influences' that can be gained through awakening the awareness of those ultimate human ends in others are so great—with all the intrinsic, literally supra-natural motivation, clarity and intensified visible and less visible effects that transformation necessarily has on all those who come into contact with each such individual and their creations—that the essential lessons to be drawn are self-evident, even if we have to follow Plato to Sicily now and again to be convinced.[50]

Of course al-Fārābī's words are not meant to convince by themselves: his serious intentions are not accessible at the level of beliefs and persuasion. Rather, they can become real or 'verified' (*muḥaqqaq*) only when we have learned to actively use them to recognise more deeply the actual workings of the human worlds all around us, and those transformations which are really possible only in those particular settings. As he tellingly points out,[51] echo-

[50] The telling story of Plato's attempts, with his companion Dion, to actualise philosophic laws and rulership in the Sicilian dictatorship of Dionysus is beautifully expressed in several of the famous *Letters* attributed to him, especially Letter VII. The authenticity of that attribution is certainly irrelevant to the philosophic lessons to be drawn here: a fascinating and equally compelling fictional dramatisation is also available in the figure of Dostoevsky's 'Grand Inquisitor' in *The Brothers Karamazov*.

[51] At *PR* 82/*N* 38, in his remarkable discussion of the 'succession' and corresponding 'happiness' of the truly virtuous founders and sustainers of the one fully human city—a passage that will recall for some the corresponding themes elaborated in Augustine's *City of God*.

ing the Qur'an, nowhere are those truly divine laws more beautifully illustrated than in the unvarying contrast, over long periods of time, between the passing influences of the visibly powerful, and the indelible traces of that secret history of what Islamic tradition calls the hidden 'friends of God' (*awliyā' Allāh*), that central concern of our next two teachers.

FROM COMMUNICATION TO COMMUNITY

We all have the remarkable fortune to live in an age when the world-wide disintegration and destruction of centuries-old forms of community and human association—often beautifully shaped, in intimate connection with small local cultures and ecological settings, by many generations of marvellous creators, spiritual, artistic and otherwise—goes hand in hand with the painful and largely invisible (because so close to each of us, and so unfinished) creative process of forging new forms of truly human community on a much wider, increasingly global geographic scale. Thus, for so many Muslims of this generation, the unavoidable challenges of creating ethically and spiritually effective communities within new nation-states (as opposed to the long-established villages, cities and tribes of so many earlier generations) must go on hand in hand with the increasingly visible incompetence of any nation–state system to deal with the global political challenges—at every level of al-Fārābī's *siyāsa*—to create what must necessarily be equally global economic, ecological, and ethically effective forms of human community.

There can hardly have been another point in human history in which the ethical challenges and creative opportunities at the focus of al-Fārābī's thought have become so visible and so unavoidable to people from every educational level and walk of life—no longer just to the educated or ruling cosmopolitan elites of so many earlier centuries, including his own. Each of our following two thinkers as well has spoken and written prophetically of this era in which the traditional, once unavoidable assumptions of 'esotericism'[52] would

[52] Of the 'elite' and the 'masses' (*khāṣṣ* and *ʿāmm*), with very different levels and forms of understanding and communication appropriate to each, as so evident throughout all the classical written forms of Islamic civilisation, not simply in al-Fārābī's works and philosophical tradition. See our *Postscript* below.

no longer be a useful, or even a feasible, premise for enabling human communication and community, of a time when more and more people might become aware that we already live in a world filled with potential 'masters', with all the new and wider responsibilities such a growing awareness entails.

In that new context, few summaries of our situation here today could be more straightforwardly objective and yet more challengingly provocative than al-Fārābī's concluding words at the very end of his long trilogy on *Attaining Happiness*:[53]

> *…therefore philosophy (the transforming love of wisdom) must necessarily come to be in each human being in the way possible for them.*

[53] There is every indication that the title *Taḥṣil al-Saʿāda* (*Attaining Happiness*: notes 12 and 24 above) is meant to be the overall title of this three-part work which has been critically edited under three separate titles. Since we had no direct access to the edited Arabic text of this final section ('The Philosophy of Aristotle') the last sentence here—which absolutely presupposes the reader's reflection on the intricate relations between all three parts of the preceding trilogy—is adapted from M. Mahdi's translation (p. 130) in his revised version, *Alfarabi's Philosophy of Plato and Aristotle* (Ithaca, Cornell University Press, 1969).

CHAPTER TWO

Ibn ʿArabī and the Tasks of Spiritual Insight and Creativity

وَجَآءَ مِنْ أَقْصَا ٱلْمَدِينَةِ رَجُلٌ يَسْعَىٰ قَالَ يَٰقَوْمِ ٱتَّبِعُوا۟ ٱلْمُرْسَلِينَ *
ٱتَّبِعُوا۟ مَن لَّا يَسْـَٔلُكُمْ أَجْرًا وَهُم مُّهْتَدُونَ *

... and there came from the farthest of the city a man running. He said: 'O my people, follow those who have been sent. Follow those who do not ask of you any reward, for they are the rightly-guided'.

Sura *Yā Sīn* (Qur'an, 36: 20-21)

WHEN WE APPROACH the writings of the great Andalusian visionary, poet, philosopher, theologian and sage Ibn ʿArabī (1165/560-1240/638) as we do here—set between the philosophic concision and rational clarity of al-Fārābī, and the immediate simplicity of Ostad Elahi's spoken spiritual advice—some of the most distinctive characteristics of his work do leap out at us. To begin with, almost everything he says is expressed in the form of some uniquely personal form of spiritual interpretation of Islamic scripture, whether the Qur'an or hadith, or of earlier Muslim interpreters of those revealed sources. An 'interpretation', to be sure, whose constantly shifting facets and multiple spiritual and intellectual perspectives are and have long remained absolutely unique and inimitable, designed to alternately shake, surprise, confront, perplex, trouble, intrigue and fascinate even the most astute and well-prepared readers. Secondly—and again this is true of virtually all his writings, certainly including the immense ocean of his magnum opus, the *Meccan Illuminations* (*al-Futūḥāt al-Makkīya*), which concerns us here—Ibn ʿArabī's expression of his ideas and intentions is boldly, unhesitatingly and quite inescapably 'esoteric'. Not simply in the most obvious sense that his real intentions and deepest meanings are carefully hidden and symbolically encrypted—for the same is surely true of the Qur'an itself—as he himself repeatedly explained in the

Introduction to this immense book.[54] But also, and far more importantly, because the built-in challenges of his unique style of writing are clearly meant to engage and transform every serious seeker, every reader who has the motivation, perspicacity, spiritual and intellectual capacities and sheer tenacity to look for the keys to these mysteries where they must always be sought. For indeed no other writing could more beautifully and thoroughly illustrate those laconic 'famous last words' of al-Fārābī with which we concluded the preceding chapter.

Despite—yet perhaps also because—of this peculiar initial difficulty, perhaps no other Islamic author has been so widely and constantly influential, over so many centuries and in so many entirely different historical and cultural settings. And Ibn ʿArabī has only become increasingly so, in more and more languages and ever wider parts of the world, in recent decades. Nor has any other author been so widely termed, with such profound respect, 'the greatest Master'.[55] This is not the occasion to explain or even to begin to outline the many reasons for those ongoing influences and their increasing role in religious thought and understanding on an ever-wider global scale.[56] And the scope of this introductory book

[54] See our translation and discussion of those key passages from his long and complex *muqaddima*, 'How to Study the *Futûhât:* Ibn 'Arabî's own Advice', pp. 73-89 in *Muhyiddin Ibn 'Arabî: 750th Anniversary Commemoration Volume*, ed. S. Hirtenstein and M. Tiernan (Shaftesbury/ Rockport, Element Books, 1993). The significance of this key passage for all readers of the *Futūḥāt* is more thoroughly developed in our essay 'Ibn 'Arabî's Rhetoric of Realisation: Keys to Reading and "Translating" the *Meccan Illuminations*', in *Journal of the Muhyiddin Ibn 'Arabi Society*, vol. XXXIII (2003), pp. 54-99 and vol. XXXIV (2004), pp. 103-145.

[55] *Al-Shaykh al-Akbar*. Even those generations of later Muslim detractors who would most strongly contest that epithet have only tended, in their own ways, to confirm the importance and powerful attraction of his ongoing and multi-faceted influence. See '*Except His Face...*: The Political and Aesthetic Dimensions of Ibn 'Arabi's Legacy', pp. 1-13 in *Journal of the Muhyiddîn Ibn 'Arabî Society*, vol. XXIII (1998); and our review of *Ibn 'Arabi and the Later Islamic Tradition: The Making of a Polemical Image in Medieval Islam*, by Alexander Knysh (Albany, SUNY Press, 1999), in the same *Journal*, vol. XXVII (2000), pp. 75-81.

[56] See especially 'Ibn 'Arabī in the "Far West": Visible and Invisible Influences', pp. 87-122 in the *Journal of the Muhyiddin Ibn 'Arabi Society*, XXIX (2001); and 'Ibn 'Arabī and His Interpreters', in *Journal of the American Oriental Society*, vol. 106 (1986), pp. 539-551 and 733-756, and vol. 107 (1987), pp. 101-119. We hope to publish soon a collected volume of these and numerous other related studies on Ibn ʿArabī's legacy and influences in both the Islamic world and the modern West.

does not allow us to properly 'introduce' Ibn ʿArabī and the major themes and intentions of his incredibly prolific writings.[57] Instead, what we propose to do here is to provide a sort of sample reading of one central theme in his *Meccan Illuminations*—expressed above all in a key chapter of the *Futūḥāt* that has particularly attracted the Shaykh's students and interpreters down through the centuries—a humanly central and practically inescapable theme which happens to be intimately connected to the particular context and purposes of this study. In order to do so, we have to begin in the middle of things, pretending to have already passed through and assimilated the thousands of dense pages of spiritual instruction—not to mention the equally essential corresponding life-experiences, practices and spiritual discoveries—which would normally have preceded an actual reader's first encounter with that long chapter.[58]

The full title of this chapter is 'Concerning the Inner Knowing of the Spiritual Waystation of the Helpers of the Mahdī appearing at the End of Time'.[59] Serious readers of Ibn ʿArabī would already have noted that this particular chapter and spiritual 'Waystation' also correspond, through a host of detailed symbolic interconnections, with the famous Sura of the Cave and its fascinating eschatological themes of the 'Sleepers' and the celebrated initiatic encounter of Moses and his mysterious, divinely inspired teacher (al-Khaḍir/'Khezr'). Thus

[57] See our new Introduction to the recent paperback edition (*Ibn ʿArabī: the Meccan Revelations*, Pir Publications, 2002) of the English-language translations, by J. Morris and W. Chittick, drawn from the bilingual anthology volume *Les Illuminations de la Mecque/The Meccan Illuminations* (Paris, Sindbad, 1989), as well as a number of helpful introductory works listed in Further Reading at the end of this book.

[58] The extent and challenging difficulties of the *Futūḥāt* are such that even a most assiduous, qualified and devoted reader would normally take years to reach chapter 366, almost three-quarters of the way through the entire work. The incomplete critical edition by O. Yahya was projected to include some forty large Arabic volumes, and an annotated English version of each of those tomes would often require two or more equally extensive volumes.

[59] Chapter 366: III, pp. 327.10-340.12. The title in Ibn ʿArabī's original 'Table of Contents' (O.Yahia, ed., I, 107) adds that '*this is from the Muhammadan Presence*'—i.e., pertaining to the universal noetic Source of all Revelation, which encompasses the spiritual 'realities' of all the historical prophets and their revelations. Readers can refer to our translation and more complete annotation of most of the central parts of chapter 366—only briefly summarized in this chapter below—in the new volume of translations from the *Futūḥāt* cited in note 57.

both Ibn ᶜArabī's title and the intimate Qur'anic correspondences of this chapter immediately raise the fundamental questions of how we should understand who is this '*mahdī*' (literally: 'the rightly-guided one'), when is 'the end of (earthly) time', and what is the significance of these mysterious 'ministers' or 'helpers' (their number as uncertain as that of the Qur'anic 'sleepers')—who are themselves not even mentioned in any of the familiar eschatological hadith with which Ibn ᶜArabī opens this chapter, yet who turn out to be the real subject of Ibn ᶜArabī's discussion at its very core.

WHO—OR WHEN, OR HOW?—IS 'RIGHTLY GUIDED'?

To begin with a bit of essential Arabic grammar and vocabulary—as one must so often do when reading and interpreting Ibn 'Arabī—the term *al-mahdī*, in its original form, is simply the passive participle of the verb *hadā*, meaning 'to lead or guide correctly, in the right direction': *al-mahdī* literally means simply 'the rightly guided person'. In the Qur'an, which here as always shapes and expresses the key parameters of Ibn 'Arabī's thought, the 'right direction' in question is always God's, and the various forms of this root occur some 330 times, indicating its centrality as one of the fundamental themes of Qur'anic teaching.[60] Yet curiously enough, the form *al-mahdī* does not occur in the Qur'an at all. Indeed it was only subsequent Islamic tradition that struggled to discover Qur'anic allusions to that messianic figure and the related actors (Jesus; the evil *dajjāl*; etc.) who are mentioned repeatedly in the eschatological dramaturgies outlined in most of the collections of hadith, and more generously embroidered in later legend.

These basic facts turn out to be quite significant when we turn to Ibn 'Arabī's treatment of 'the Mahdī' in the *Futūḥāt*. For in fact the word '*al-mahdī*' occurs throughout that vast book only 33 times, and all but eight of those mentions are included here in chapter 366.[61]

[60] The centrality of that concept becomes even more evident if we also include the occurrences (19 times) of forms of the closely related Arabic root *r-sh-d*.

[61] After chapter 366 there is only one final allusion in chapter 557 (IV, 195, on the 'Absolute Seal of the Saints' [=Jesus]), simply referring the reader to Ibn ᶜArabī's detailed discussion of the spiritual rank of Jesus (as 'Seal') and his eschatological relations to the Mahdi in his own earlier *K. 'Anqā' Mughrib* (now available in the

And when we examine the ways Ibn ʿArabī uses the same term on the seven occasions where he does mention it prior to this chapter, something very interesting begins to emerge. On each of those occasions, this expression (*al-mahdī*) is used in an entirely *non*-technical sense: not as a sort of honorific title or distinctive form of address (as it usually appears in the eschatological hadith that are the initial apparent subject of chapter 366), but instead in the more ordinary sense of *any person* who is spiritually 'rightly guided', who has received and actively assimilated some degree of inner divine guidance in various realms of life.

Now this distinctive method of deconstructing an overly fossilised, routinised technical term or religious symbol, by returning to its deeper etymological roots and to the network of subtle spiritual meanings almost always potentially present in the original Qur'anic Arabic, is of course familiar to every student of Ibn ʿArabī. Here, as in many of those other cases, he is using that same rhetorical method to turn his perceptive readers' attention toward the *existential, real meanings* of the underlying 'Reality'—in this case, each person's experiential 'unveilings' of the manifestations (*tajalliyāt*) and necessarily unique discoveries of the divine Name *al-Hādī* ('the Guide'). Moreover, the way that these carefully distributed uses of that term in preceding chapters would eventually orient the carefully attentive reader who actually follows Ibn ʿArabī through the *Futūḥāt* do vividly illustrate the usefulness—if not indeed the necessity—of following the Shaykh's own slow, explicitly 'scattered' method of writing and revealing his deepest intentions.[62]

'WAITING FOR THE MAHDI'?

In this case, that preceding focus on the wider, spiritual meanings of someone's being 'rightly guided' inevitably creates a peculiar kind

---

English translation by G. Elmore, Brill, 1999). The other seven—all non-'technical'— uses of the term '*al-mahdī*' preceding chapter 366 are in chapters 36, 72 (twice), chapter 73, and 365 (twice).

[62] See the key passages in this regard from the Prologue to the *Futūhāt* brought together and translated in our article cited in n. 54 above. We have carefully illustrated and explored Ibn ʿArabī's actual use of this method of 'scattering' his most essential teachings in a number of thematic studies of the *Futūḥāt* which should soon appear in *The Reflective Heart: Discovering Spiritual Intelligence in Ibn ʿArabī's*

of shock when the reader suddenly first encounters the mysterious—but often quite vividly detailed—discussions of 'the Mahdi' as a very specific messianic character in the hadith that are quoted at length in the opening pages of chapter 366. But that initial puzzlement is surely magnified and compounded when we then move on to Ibn 'Arabī's strange discussions of the spiritual gifts of the Mahdi's 'ministers' or 'helpers' (*wuzarā'*: themselves not even mentioned in the actual hadith) which take up most of the remainder of this long chapter.[63] To put it as simply as possible—which means setting aside for the moment the complex and highly subtle rhetorical tools Ibn 'Arabī uses to raise and pursue these questions—the thoughtful and well-prepared reader who has already navigated through some two-thirds of this immense work is now rapidly forced to consider three basic alternatives.

Is Ibn 'Arabī talking here about a particular militarily powerful, charismatic political figure—as described in the 'obvious' sense of the hadith—who will appear at some remotely distant 'end of time' (*ākhir al-zamān*, as the chapter title has it)? In that case *al-Mahdī* here is the title of a specific historical individual (whether mythical or otherwise), and the actual spiritual relevance of such speculations for most readers—and more importantly, to the actual existential meanings of divine 'Guidance' in their own lives—is apparently rather remote, fascinating and curious though such apocalyptic speculations might appear for some.

A second possibility, which at least brings the discussions in this chapter closer to the existential concerns and responsibilities of Ibn 'Arabī's readers, is to shift the time-frame within which one reads both these prophecies (from the hadith) and Ibn 'Arabī's subsequent interpretations and elaborations sharply towards the present

'Meccan Illuminations' and several subsequent volumes: see Further Reading below.

[63] *Futūḥāt*, vol. III, pp. 327-340; the discussion of hadith (mixed with some powerful personal anecdotes) takes up roughly the first four long Arabic pages of this chapter, and Ibn 'Arabī's even more enigmatic and puzzling list of the distinctive gifts of divine 'knowledges' (*'ulūm*) characterising this particular spiritual stage cover more than two pages of Arabic text at the end of the chapter. We might add that the density of the printed Arabic text and its contents is such that serious translation and the necessary commentary and explanation of a single page normally demands a dozen or more pages in Western languages.

or the immediately impending future—but still entirely on the this-worldly, historical plane. The reader's focus in this case is turned toward an understanding of the Mahdi's impending reign of justice as a much more immediate political and religious imperative. In that context, Ibn 'Arabī's discussions of the Mahdi's 'Helpers' and advisors could appear as possible allusions to the conditions for bringing about a hoped-for radical transformation of this-worldly political and social arrangements—perhaps even to the roles of particular individuals (including Ibn 'Arabī himself?) in this prophesied transformation.[64] It is important to note that there were ample historical antecedents for that kind of limited politico-religious perspective on the 'mahdī' in Ibn 'Arabī's own Islamic milieu, both in his own time (especially in Andalusia and the Maghreb) and in earlier and later periods.[65] And in particular, the vividly anti-clerical rhetoric of much of this chapter has been echoed in popular messianic movements, tensions and expectations far beyond the Islamic world as well.[66]

Since the wider messianic resonances of this language—and the

[64] Chapter 366 is the site of some of Ibn 'Arabī's most open allusions to his self-conception as 'Seal of the Muhammadan Saints' and to his unique relationship with the Qur'an and its Source (further elaborated in the following chapter 367: see our translation and commentary in 'The Spiritual Ascension: Ibn 'Arabî and the Mi'râj', in *Journal of the American Oriental Society*, vol. 107 (1987), pp. 629-652, and vol. 108 (1988), pp. 63-77). Chapter 366 also contains some striking anecdotes about contemporary Sufi acquaintances of his who are presented as embodying various characteristics of the Mahdi's Helpers.

[65] The central political terms of his discussion in this chapter (*imām*, *ḥujja*, and *mahdī* itself) all had powerful, explicitly historical and political connotations in earlier widely influential Shiʿi movements and writings: we may mention in particular the *Rasā'il* of the Ikhwān al-Ṣafā', whose distinctive language is sometimes literally echoed in the expressions used here. Most dramatically, the famous 19th-century 'Mahdi' of the Sudan quite literally followed in detail the division of *wuzarā'* and their functions set forth in this chapter, while Ibn Khaldūn's vigorous criticisms of supposed 'millenarian' tendencies and teachings in Ibn 'Arabī and their ostensible historical influences in Africa are a notorious leitmotif throughout his *Muqaddima*: see our chapter on *An Arab "Machiavelli"? : Rhetoric, Philosophy and Politics in Ibn Khaldun's Critique of Sufism*, to appear in the proceedings of the Harvard Ibn Khaldun Conference (ed. Roy Mottahedeh).

[66] See especially our detailed study, originally prepared as a commentary on this chapter 366, of 'Ibn 'Arabî's "Esotericism": The Problem of Spiritual Authority', pp. 37-64 in *Studia Islamica*, LXXI (1990).

standard historical, religious and metaphysical assumptions that underlie them—are everywhere familiar in the history of religions, we can quickly summarise some of the ramifications and eventual weaknesses of either of these interpretive options. Because both of these possible Islamic understandings of the Mahdi are closely echoed by perennial tendencies in Jewish and Christian apocalyptic thought and expectation (and in those latter cases, by ostensibly 'secular' messianic variants of those beliefs that violently ravaged much of the globe over the past century), the weaknesses, pitfalls and dangers—both worldly and spiritual—of both options are all too apparent. Either one is left 'waiting for the Mahdi' and his far-off reign of divine justice, while the present age cycles downward into deeper and deeper chaos. Or one could turn more actively to the sort of overt political 'preparation' for that revolutionary epiphany, an approach whose actually recurrent worldly consequences, over the centuries, are and have been evident enough to anyone who cares to look.

Now in the larger context of what we know of Ibn 'Arabī's life and his writings, neither of those interpretive options seems very persuasive. Of course, one cannot 'disprove' such messianic interpretations—especially since each has so clearly had its own historical proponents in later Islamic contexts—but at the very least, they seem to raise all sorts of apparent contradictions. In particular, within the context of chapter 366 itself, each of these first two interpretations highlights a particularly puzzling contradiction: why this sudden emphasis on the unique role in religious guidance of one particularly privileged historical individual—whose political role and defining characteristics are curiously parallel to those of the Prophet Muhammad, though in an indeterminate and brief future time (reigning at most for nine years)—when everything else in these *Meccan Illuminations* (and indeed throughout Ibn 'Arabī's writings more generally) emphasises the universality and *immediate presence* of the inspiration of the Qur'an and the universal noetic 'Reality of Muhammad', and the corresponding responsibility (and spiritual necessity) of every individual human being to seek out and begin to realise that omnipresent reality of divine 'Guidance'?[67]

[67] Any adequate commentary on chapter 366 would require a detailed discussion

BECOMING 'RIGHTLY-GUIDED'

This last question brings us directly to the third possible interpretation of Ibn 'Arabī's intentions in chapter 366: the possibility that the *al-mahdī*, the 'rightly guided one' in question here, far from referring to some particularly effective warrior and chieftain, is precisely—if only potentially at first—*each* properly prepared reader (and actor) who begins to realise that Guidance in action. That is, the 'rightly guided person' is whoever, by actualising that divine guidance, begins to become—or to truly 'know'—the *Imām al-waqt*, the 'Guide-of-the-present-instant,' as Ibn 'Arabī mysteriously describes that figure throughout the central sections of this chapter. Far from being a particular historical group of actors, like each prophet and his initial supporters, those familiar messianic terms and stories are translated here into the facets or stages of a single repeated process of spiritual transformation. Thus, actualising the distinctive spiritual qualities of these 'Helpers'—as Ibn 'Arabī describes each of those attributes here in detail—necessarily begins to make one 'rightly guided' (*mahdī*), and by the same token makes one a *living* guide and model (the literal meaning of *imām al-waqt* and *al-imām al-mahdī*) for all those with whom one interacts. We only have to look at Ibn 'Arabī's own life and work—and its ongoing and fascinatingly far-reaching influences—to see precisely how that ongoing process of spiritual guidance actively operates. Indeed, as he constantly points out, we can only really ever 'see' as much of that eschatological process as we have already begun to realise for ourselves.

Moreover, this is a process of essential orientation, as Ibn 'Arabī and the Qur'an alike insist, that ultimately engages *every* human being. Without that inner divine guidance—which is what alone can make us truly and fully human (*insān*)—each person[68] is necessarily

---

of all the related passages echoing the profusion of central Qur'anic themes and symbols in the corresponding Sura of the Cave. We do not yet have such a parallel commentary, even at a relatively superficial level, for any of these lengthy chapters in Ibn ʿArabī's 'Section on the Spiritual Waystations' (*faṣl al-manāzil*: chapters 270-383), each of which is intricately connected with the successive corresponding Suras of the Qur'an, beginning with the final Sura (for chapter 270).

[68] Or rather, each *bashar*, the mortal 'human-animal' which is the actual state of most.

'guided' instead by the familiar constantly shifting combination of their inner impulses and fears, together with their even more unstable particular milieu of social and cultural programming. Within the individual and in larger social and cultural groupings alike, both those sorts of purported 'guidance' are of course in constant, never-ending conflict, disorder and states of change. Yet it is precisely those providentially arranged perpetual conflicts which eventually lead people to seek out and discover—and then creatively translate into practice—that genuine Guidance which moves them toward the perception and eventual realisation of a wholly different kind of order.[69]

Seen from that all-inclusive perspective, chapter 366 thus turns out to be a kind of epitome of the entire *Futūḥāt*—or rather, a decisive point at which each responsible reader is openly challenged to begin to 'translate' its practical spiritual teachings, so carefully summarised there, into the kind of effectively and appropriately realised practice that is itself, in Ibn 'Arabī's perspective, the constantly repeated 'end of time' stressed in his title.[70] For each instant of inspired awareness of that divine spiritual guidance takes place quite literally 'beyond earthly-time' and simultaneously returns to that trans-temporal realm as the lasting spiritual 'fruits'—this eschatological symbolism is centrally Qur'anic—of our purified intention and all rightly guided actions flowing from that enlightened awareness.

DISCOVERING GOD'S 'HELP' AND THE SOUL'S 'DESTINED TIME'

This conception of our trans-historical destiny and emergence as

[69] See the initial development of this theme in our Introduction and Chapter One above, and Ostad Elahi's further amplification in the following Chapter Three.

[70] *ākhir al-zamān*. We have placed this phrase in quote marks to highlight the fact that Ibn 'Arabī, throughout many earlier passages of the *Futūḥāt*, has constantly stressed (a) the ultimately 'unreal' and—from a phenomenological and experiential perspective—almost infinitely flexible nature of our perceptions of this 'relative time' (*zamān*). And (b) the contrast of our 'imagined reality' of *zamān* with the true knowers' enlightened awareness of the actual reality of the divine 'Moment' (*waqt*) and its ontological 'root' in the divine Name *al-Dahr*—closest to 'the Tao', since neither 'Destiny' nor 'Eternity' [the usual translation equivalents] come close to conveying the infinitely varying divine creativity and Self-transformation that are essential to what this term actually conveys for Ibn 'Arabī. See the excellent summary of the relevant concepts and passages in the *Futūḥāt* by G. Böwering, 'Ibn 'Arabî's Concept of Time', in *Gott ist schön und Er liebt die Schönheit*, ed. A. Giese and J.C. Bürgel (Peter Lang, Bern, 1994), pp. 71-91.

a truly spiritual human being (*insān*) which Ibn 'Arabī develops more fully here in chapter 366 is already dramatically foreshadowed in his discussion of each individual's 'end of time' in chapter 274.[71] That chapter and its specific spiritual stage correspond to the Shaykh's spiritual exegesis of the innermost meanings of the dramatically eschatological Sura *al-Naṣr* (110), the same Sura which concludes this book. The title of this chapter is also explicitly eschatological: 'Concerning the Inner Knowing of the Waystation of the "Appointed Time" (*al-'ajal al-musammā*)', a recurrent Qur'anic expression ordinarily understood to refer to the chronological time of bodily death. However, Ibn 'Arabī pointedly and unambiguously stresses here that this expression can in fact *only* refer to the moment of each individual's true spiritual 'Awakening' (*baᶜth*: a central eschatological term in the Qur'an), an awareness so beautifully and perennially expressed in the powerful vision of the corresponding Sura of the Cave. Then he quickly moves on to a marvellous phenomenological description of that awakening process, clearly referring to his own personal experiences and those of his own spiritual companions. He describes that decisive spiritual awakening, in a kind of technical shorthand, as 'the Greatest Providence' (*al-ᶜināyat al-kubrā*), where *ᶜināya* refers specifically—and much more personally and directly than the abstract 'providence' in English—to God's attentively 'watching over' and taking intimate, personal care of all things, especially the individual spiritual destiny of each human soul.

> Know, O listener, that the people of God, when the Real One (*al-Ḥaqq*) draws them toward Himself, He places in their hearts something calling them to seek their (true) happiness. So they seek after that and inquire about it until they find in their hearts a certain tenderness and humility, and striving for peace and release from the state of ordinary people with their (normal conditions of) mutual envy, greed, hostility and opposition.
>
> Then when they have completed the perfection of their moral qualities, or have nearly done so, they find within themselves[72] some-

[71] *Futūḥāt* II, 587-590.

[72] Literally, in their *nafs*: Ibn 'Arabī's stress here on the unreliable intuitions and

thing calling them toward solitary retreat and withdrawal from ordinary people. So some of them take to wandering (*siyāḥa*) and frequenting the (wild) mountains and plains, while others do their wandering between the towns and cities—moving from one to another as soon as they've come to know and get used to the people of a particular place—while still others isolate themselves in a room in their own homes, staying there alone and cut off from people. All of that is so that they can be alone and at ease with the Real One (*al-Ḥaqq*) who has called them to Him—not in order to find any particular being or miraculous event, whether sensible or in their innermost selves.[73]

Thus all of those we have mentioned continue like that until they are suddenly illuminated by something from God that comes between them and their *nafs*—which for some of them occurs in their *nafs*; for others in their imagination (*khiyāl*: = dreams, visions, etc.); and for others from outside themselves. Then they are suddenly filled with longing because of that occurrence, and they immediately seek the company of (other human) creatures... Now there comes to them through that occurrence a (divine) 'addressing' and informing them of their state or of what (God) is calling them to, as with...[74]

Then they are granted inner ease and satisfaction wherever they are. But all of this (comfort after their loneliness) is only a test (*ibtilā'*), unless God gives them comfort with (the company) of the angelic spirits of light. For this (alone) will bring about their spiritually successful labour (*falāḥ*), indeed verifies and realises it. And this (alone) is 'the good news (*bushrā*) from God' through which God's

sentiments of the lower *nafs*, which require further careful discernment—rather than the purified theophanic Heart (*al-qalb*)—is quite significant.

[73] This recurrent spiritual process and wider 'phenomenology' of spiritual learning it entails, only briefly recalled here, are more fully developed in a number of other key passages from the *Futūḥāt* and other writings partially translated and presented in our article '*He moves you through the Land and Sea...*: Learning from the Earthly Journey', pp. 1-30 in *Journal of the Muhyiddîn Ibn 'Arabî Society*, vol. XVII (1996), to appear more fully in our planned volume of thematically related translations *The Traveler and the Way: 'Wandering' and the Spiritual Journey*.

[74] Here Ibn ʿArabī gives at some length the stories of the decisive moment of illumination of several famous Sufis, such as Ibrahīm ibn Adham's being out hunting when a deer tells him '*You weren't created for this!*' Or of other Sufis who heard a voice saying: '*If you were to seek Me, you would lose Me at the first step*', or '*You are My servant.*'

Providence has come rushing to them in this way. As for anything else, it is an enormous danger, and they should struggle to separate from it. [But if the person favoured with this enlightenment perseveres,] then the (angelic) spirits continue to accompany them in the world of their imagination during most of their states, and even appear to them in sensible form at certain times. They shouldn't make an effort (to hold on) to that or to avoid it, but rather work to deepen their connection with that (source of inspiration) and to acquire the spiritual benefit that comes from it. For *that* is what must be sought.

So if (such a person) hears a (divine) address '*from behind the veil*' of their *nafs*, they should '*give heed, while He is witnessing*', and remember what they were hearing.[75] If that (divine) speaking requires a reply in accordance with the extent of your understanding, then respond as far as you understand. For if you are given (divine) knowing about that (appropriate creative response), then that *is* 'the Greatest Providence.'[76]

THE 'GREATEST PROVIDENCE' AND THE TASK OF SPIRITUAL COMMUNICATION

This initial allusion to the decisive spiritual illumination that is 'the Greatest Providence' is further elaborated in chapter 315,[77] where Ibn 'Arabī explains more openly his own personal mission and the specific qualities his readers and students need in order to benefit from his teaching:

[75] This famous verse (41:52) is at the heart of Ibn 'Arabī's discussion of the distinctive spiritual attainments of the Mahdi's 'Helpers' in chapter 366, especially in the second of those qualities of spiritual receptivity outlined below ('The Qualities of Spiritual Receptivity'). See also Ibn ʿArabī's many further developments of these key Qur'anic passages on our awareness of God, translated and discussed in our 'Listening For God: Prayer and the Heart in the Futûhât', pp. 19-53 in *Prayer of the Heart*, ed. J. Mercer (Berkeley/Oxford, MIAS, 1993); to be included in revised form in our forthcoming *The Reflective Heart: Discovering Spiritual Intelligence in Ibn 'Arabî's 'Meccan Illuminations'*.

[76] But if you don't understand immediately what to do with such a direct divine message, Ibn ʿArabī continues, then remember it and wait until God reveals the proper moment and response.

[77] III, 57-60, on the 'Spiritual Waystation of the Inner Knowing of the Necessity of Suffering (*wujūb al-ʿidhāb*)', corresponding to another openly eschatological Sura, *al-ḥashr* (59). The short quotation here is from vol. III, the bottom of p. 58 and top of p. 59.

> For we are not 'messengers from God' until we fulfil our responsibility to convey these kinds of spiritual knowing by communicating them.[78] And we only mention what we do mention of them for those who have both true faith and intelligence (*al-mu'minīn al-ʿuqalā'*), who are constantly occupied with purifying their souls together with God and who constantly oblige their souls to realise [*taḥaqquq*: the subject of this book] the humility of servanthood and their needfulness for God in all of their states. Then (for such individuals) the Light of God *is* their inner vision (*baṣīra*), either through knowing (from God) or through true faith and surrender to what has come to them in the reports from God and His Books and Messengers. For that (active spiritual receptivity) is the Greatest Providence, the closest place (to God), the most perfect path and the greatest happiness. May God bring us together with those who are of this description!

Needless to say, some such special providence has certainly continued to bring Ibn 'Arabī's writings and influence together with readers and creators of that rare description, down through many centuries. And passages such as those we have just quoted—which, taken together, give such an extraordinary phenomenological description of what is always involved in discovering and then actualising the divine 'Guidance' (*hudā*, etc.), or in other words, of gradually becoming '*al-mahdī*'—together make up a great proportion of his *Meccan Illuminations*. So such properly qualified readers would not likely be too puzzled when they encounter in chapter 366 the strange transition from the familiar hadith descriptions of the Mahdi, to the 'Imam-Mahdi' (or simply the 'Imam of the moment'), and then to his requisite spiritual qualities exemplified by the figures of his mysterious emblematic 'Helpers'. The announced subject of this chapter, after all, is '*the inner knowing of the spiritual* waystation (*manzil*) of the rightly-guided one.' It is not billed as some sort of 'history lesson in advance'. And demanding as those corresponding requirements might be, the actual realisation of that spiritual

[78] Ibn 'Arabī's reference here is specifically to the importance of our communicating the subject of this chapter, the deeper spiritual necessity of suffering, because, as he goes on to explain, unenlightened people find this basic reality of earthly existence virtually impossible to understand on an existential level, while '*the (spiritual) knowers have a vast capacity for this*'.

station, as Ibn 'Arabī describes it here, is surely the unavoidable responsibility of every human being seeking right Guidance, whatever their particular circumstances may be.

TRANSFORMATION AND THE 'END' OF *EARTHLY* 'TIME'

Indeed even the initial realisation of that spiritual station in itself already begins to transform those apparent circumstances, bringing about the dramatic 'end' of earthbound, terrestrial time (*al-zamān*) for anyone who becomes even remotely aware of the realities and actual extent of the spiritual worlds. In fact, the attentive reader could not help being struck quite forcefully by the mysterious addition of a single key term in the chapter title at this point, compared with the version of that title given in Ibn 'Arabī's original Table of Contents (*fihris*) at the beginning of the *Futūḥāt*. Instead of speaking simply of 'the Mahdi at the end of time described by the Prophet'—which sounds like a boring summary of what was already given in the original hadith—Ibn 'Arabī here adds, and thereby strongly highlights, the key qualifier 'who is appearing, becoming manifest' (*al-Ẓāhir*) at the end of earthly time. As if to say: our real subject is precisely this *ẓuhūr*, this ongoing process and reality of divine inspiration and manifestation, in the very heart of our earthly existence.

What is so strikingly emphasized in that subtly new title is precisely its explicit emphasis on the ongoing, perennial task of realising and actualising that spiritual guidance. Whoever begins to do so, Ibn ʿArabī implies, has already become an 'Imam' (a spiritual leader and model) and a further source of spiritual guidance—and simultaneously comes to embody a pointed, unavoidable challenge, as he constantly re-emphasises almost brutally throughout this chapter, to all those falsely claiming or presuming wider authority for their own imagined forms of guidance, interpretation and pseudo-knowledge. Particularly important in this regard are his detailed discussions at the end of this same chapter on the severe divine restrictions which the Qur'an imposes on any sort of pointless 'disputation' or propagandising with those who are not spiritually properly prepared to benefit from the inspired knower's illuminations.[79]

[79] See, for example, the following key passage:

> And this spiritual waystation includes the knowing of what sort of arguing (con-

The '*mahdī*', in this sense, is a Reality that always exists—whatever names might be given to that Reality (the 'Imam' is the epithet repeatedly emphasised here)—and which is therefore always accessible to those who would care to seek. The situation of that Reality is not simply analogous to the equally mysterious role of the 'Seals' of sainthood (that is, of *walāya*: spiritual 'proximity' to God, and everything which flows from that) elsewhere in the *Futūḥāt*.[80] In reality, all those terms may actually refer to the same spiritual Source, as Ibn 'Arabī strongly hints at several autobiographical passages or allusions in this same chapter. In this case, as with the mystery of the two 'Seals', it makes no sense to pose the question as referring either to some particular historical figure or to a trans-historical Reality. For everything in his metaphysics of divine Self-manifestations or theophanies (*tajalliyāt*)—or of the eternal 'spiritual realities' (*rūḥānīyāt*) and their changing earthly 'representatives' (*nā'ib*), where particular spiritual personalities and their perennial functions are concerned[81]—points to the fact that those Realities can only be known through their manifestations.

---

cerning the practice and principles of religion) is praiseworthy and what sort is to be condemned. Someone who has (truly) surrendered (to God) among those who depend on God should not argue except concerning what he has had confirmed and realised (through God) by way of inner unveiling, *not* on the basis of (his own) thinking and inquiry. So if he has actually witnessed (as an direct inspiration from God) that about which they are arguing, then in that event it is incumbent on him to argue about it using *that which is better* (29:46)— provided that he has been specifically ordered to do so by a divine command.

But if he does not have a divine command to do so, then the choice is up to him. Thus if the task of helping the other person (by convincing him of) that (revealed insight) has been assigned to him (by God), then he has been entrusted with that mission for him. But if he despairs of his listeners' ever accepting what he has to say, then he should shut up and not argue. For if he should argue (with no real hope of affecting his listeners), then he is (really) striving to bring about their perdition with God…

80 Although Ibn ʿArabī's important self-conception of this distinctive spiritual role is clearly discussed in each of the excellent recent biographies mentioned in Further Reading below, by far the most comprehensive treatment of this key subject is to be found in M. Chodkiewicz' *Le Sceau des saints* (and the English translation), both mentioned in the bibliographic section below.

81 Again, see the detailed illustrations and invaluable explanations of this central theme of 'sainthood' and the spiritual hierarchy throughout M. Chodkiewicz' *The Seal of the Saints* (in Further Reading below).

INTRODUCING THE MAHDI'S 'HELPERS'

After a long quotation and summary of various hadith describing the Mahdī, Ibn ʿArabī suddenly adds, without any break or suggestion that he is still not quoting or paraphrasing those hadith, the following description of this figure's 'ministers' or 'Helpers':[82]

> He will have divine men upholding his call (to the true Religion) and aiding him in his victory; they are the Helpers. They will bear the burdens of (his) government and help him to carry out all the details of what God has imposed on him...
>
> God will appoint as his Helpers a group (of people) whom He has kept hidden for him in the secret recesses of His Unseen (i.e., the spiritual world). God has acquainted (these Helpers), through unveiling and immediate witnessing, with the realities and the contents of God's Command concerning His servants. So the Mahdi makes his decisions and judgements on the basis of consultation with them, since they are the true Knowers who really know what is There...
>
> Among the secrets of the knowledge of the Mahdi's Helpers whom God has appointed as ministers for him is His saying: '*The victorious support of the people of faith is obligatory for Us*' (30:47), for they follow in the footsteps of those among the Companions who sincerely fulfilled what they had pledged to God. These Helpers are from the non-Arab peoples; none of them is Arab, although they speak only Arabic... *So his Helpers are the guides* (*al-hudāt*), while he is the rightly-guided one (*al-mahdī*). And this is the extent of what the Mahdī attains of the knowledge of God, with the aid of his Helpers.

Then Ibn ʿArabī goes on to describe the core spiritual qualities, accomplishments and forms of inspired knowing associated with this particular spiritual stage, connecting his hesitant numbering of those distinctive spiritual virtues with the purposefully vague 'number' of the Helpers, while also alluding to the mysterious Qur'anic account of the disputed number of Sleepers in the narrative

[82] The brief selections given throughout the remainder of this chapter are greatly abridged from our longer, fully annotated version of those key passages included in the recently published anthology volume *The Meccan Revelations* (section on 'The End of Time'): see details in Further Reading below.

of the corresponding Sura of the Cave (18):

> ...Now I do know what (spiritual qualities) are needed by the Mahdi's Helper. So if there is only one Helper, then everything he needs is united in that one person, and if they are more than one, then there are not more than nine of them, since that was the limit of the uncertainty the Messenger of God expressed in his saying concerning the rule of the Mahdi, that it was 'for five, seven or nine years.' And the totality of what he needs to have performed for him by his Helpers are nine things; there is not a tenth, nor can they be any fewer...

THE SPIRITUAL QUALITIES OF THE HELPERS[83]

Ibn 'Arabi then briefly enumerates the nine characteristics described in detail in the rest of this chapter, and again insists that all nine of these qualities are required by the Helpers, no matter what their exact number may be. However, the Helpers themselves are not mentioned in the rest of the chapter, where these different spiritual attributes are instead attributed directly to the entirely new figure (or figures?) of 'the Imam', 'Imam of the Age', 'Rightly-guided Imam', etc.—or else to the saints (*awliyā'*), the accomplished 'Friends of God' more generally. Perhaps especially important is his insistence at the very end of this long discussion that these characteristic spiritual qualities and abilities can only become manifest, at least in their completely adequate form, in various individuals—in other words, that the full realisation and earthly manifestation of these equally essential spiritual qualities may be necessarily collective or co-operative by its very nature:

> Now these nine things are not combined all together for any Imam among the leaders of Religion and the vice-regents of God and His Prophet until the Day of the Rising, except for this Rightly-guided Imam...

It soon becomes clear that the nine distinctive spiritual qualities of these 'Helpers' (or the 'Imam') discussed in detail in this central section of chapter 366 all have to do either with (a) the 'reception'

[83] *Futūḥāt* III, 331.34-338.2; see the complete translations and fuller commentary included in *The Meccan Revelations* anthology.

and comprehension of divine guidance (the first three qualities); or else (b) with the further 'translation' of that guidance into effective action and responsible spiritual communication and guidance of others (the last six). Far from being unique to a single historically future 'Mahdi' and his putative advisors, all nine of those spiritual qualities are clearly illustrated, at the very least, in what each reader will already know of the lives and teachings of many of the prophets and saints, whatever the particular religious tradition and sacred history in question.

But before we begin to outline Ibn ʿArabī's description of each of those qualities, let us stop and take notice of something much more important: what Ibn ʿArabī has, rather surreptitiously, actually done to his readers at this point. For his approach to these qualities is neither a personal 'interpretation' of Islamic scriptural (or other Sufi) sources; nor is it a personal 'teaching' about these particular qualities in themselves. What he has in fact provided for each reader here is to set up a very complex, peculiarly interactive mirror for their own spiritual life and experiences—including all the different planes and sources and 'verifications' of those experiences, both '*in their souls*' and '*on the horizons*'[84]—precisely as each of those nine qualities is actualised, intimated or at least foreshadowed in their own uniquely individual development.

This sort of powerfully probing 'mirroring' takes place throughout the *Futūḥāt*, but rarely do we find such far-reaching, spiritually essential issues so openly at stake and so carefully and sometimes passionately described. Since any detailed discussion and explanation of Ibn ʿArabī's often tightly condensed formulae here could easily become a book of its own, we have judged it best simply to translate only the most essential parts of these phenomenological accounts, leaving it to each reader—as Ibn 'Arabī himself does—to provide their own concrete personal illustrations.

THE QUALITIES OF SPIRITUAL RECEPTIVITY

Before turning to Ibn ʿArabī's actual descriptions of these seven essential spiritual qualities, it is important to make explicit one indispensable piece of background information which even the

[84] See 41:53, the famous verse concluding our Introduction above.

novice reader of the *Futūḥāt* (or of Ibn ʿArabī's even more widely known *Bezels of Wisdom*, the *Fuṣūs al-Ḥikam*) would certainly have fully assimilated long before reaching this chapter. That is his distinctive conception, deeply rooted in the Qur'an, of all of creation—and therefore of all conceivable human experience—as never-repeated divine 'Signs' or 'theophanies,' as the infinite, constantly changing Self-manifestation of all the divine Names or Attributes. His works, of course, are intended not to transmit some superficial philosophical 'theory' or theological 'belief' in such symbolic notions, but rather to communicate and awaken each reader's immediate inner awareness of this reality, which only very slowly comes into focus and full consciousness—and to do so precisely through the ongoing contrast between our normally unconscious states of spiritual 'heedlessness' and the memorable moments of inspired awareness of this deeper reality of things.

The short selections that follow are striking illustrations of his typical rhetorical methods for suggesting, highlighting and gradually awakening this indispensable dimension of unfolding spiritual awareness. In each case, he first presents his readers with a scriptural phrase or allusion that seems to apply only to the great prophets, saints and far-off paragons of spiritual virtue. But that seemingly familiar verse or hadith is quickly followed, in each case, by a kind of unexpected metaphysical 'punch-line' which suddenly forces his readers to reconsider and reflect much more deeply on all the previously hidden (or as yet unconceived) ways in which that scriptural allusion or spiritual realisation might actually apply to themselves.

> (1) As for 'penetrating vision', that is so his (i.e., the helper's or rightly-guided one's) *calling upon God* may be *with (clear) inward vision* (12:108) concerning what he is requesting in his prayer... So he regards the inner essence of each (divine aspect or 'Name')[85] to Whom he is praying and sees what is possible for (that divine aspect) to do in response to his prayer; then he prays to Him for that...

[85] Ibn ʿArabī's expression here apparently refers to his characteristic understanding that each person's innermost strivings or petitions to God—i.e., 'prayer' in the broadest possible sense, whether or not consciously or verbally, formally formulated as such—necessarily are directed toward one or another specific aspects of the overall divine Reality, expressed in Qur'anic terms by the many divine

If this spiritual quality might at first seem impossibly difficult and remote, Ibn ʿArabī goes on to describe other manifestations of that same 'penetrating vision' which are clearly inseparable from the most elementary levels of everyone's spiritual insight and awareness, for which *any* reader can supply dramatic personal examples, from spiritual dreams and intuitions to all the manifestations of what Ibn ʿArabī elsewhere describes as the ever-deepening recognition of all of existence as a mysterious divine 'shadow-theatre':[86]

> ... And it is also (characteristic) of this penetrating vision that if the spiritual meanings take on bodily form, then that person recognises (the underlying realities) in those very forms, and they know without any hesitation which spiritual meaning it is that became embodied (in that particular form).

The next form of spiritual receptivity Ibn ʿArabī mentions begins with a well-known verse of the Qur'an which is normally understood to speak of the highest and rarest forms of theophany, the familiar illustrations of each of the great prophets and divine Messengers. But in this case, he quickly makes clear that his central concern is actually the obscuring 'veils'—and the corresponding 'unveilings' and inspirations—which are far more intimate and familiar to each of us than we might at first want to admit:

> (2) Now as for 'understanding the divine address when it is delivered',[87] this is (summarised) in His saying: '*And it was not for any mortal (bashar) that God should speak to him except through inspiration or from behind a veil or He sends a messenger*' (42:51)... So as for

Names ('Lord', 'King', 'All-Compassionate', etc.), that constitute the ontological 'lord' and 'sustainer' (*rabb*) of that particular individual at that instant.

[86] See the full translation and discussion of that famous image of the 'Divine Comedy' (from chapter 317 of the *Futūḥāt*) in our article 'Seeing Past the Shadows: Ibn 'Arabî's "Divine Comedy"', pp. 50-69 in *Journal of the Muhyiddîn Ibn 'Arabî Society*, XII (1993).

[87] Here the divine 'address' (*al-khiṭāb al-ilāhī*) or 'discourse' is the divine 'Speech' (*kalām/ḥadīth*) specifically as it is directed toward—and received by—a particular person. Its 'delivery' or transmission (*ilqā'*: literally 'projection') into the heart (or hearing, or any other spiritual senses) of the person thus addressed may take any of the forms described later in this passage (only partially translated here)—since ultimately (for Ibn ʿArabī, but relying on many passages of the Qur'an) *all Being is nothing but divine 'Speech.*

the divine address '*through inspiration*', that is what He delivers to their hearts as something newly reported (to them), so that through this they gain knowledge of some particular matter… And as for His saying '*or from behind a veil*', that is a divine address delivered to the (person's) hearing and not to the heart, so that the person to whom it is delivered perceives it and then understands from that what was intended by the One Who caused them to hear it. Sometimes that happens through the forms of theophany (*tajalli*, 'divine Self-manifestation'), in which case that divine form addresses the person, and that form itself is the 'veil'. In that case (the person having this spiritual insight) understands from that divine address the knowledge of what it indicates, and they know that (this theophanic form) is a veil and that the Speaker (i.e., God) is behind that veil.

And again this is followed by the sudden 'punch-line', the sort of metaphysical formula meant to leave each of his readers reflecting, recalling, and re-examining so many dimensions of our most everyday experience of the world:

Of course not everyone who perceives a form of the divine theophany realises that that form is God. For the person possessing this state (of spiritual insight) is only distinguished from other people by the fact that he recognises that that form, although it is a 'veil,' is itself precisely God's theophany for him.

The third quality of spiritual receptivity introduced here, however, is described in such terms that everyone who has ever 'created', whatever the form of art or performance in question, will immediately recognize the sort of inspiration to which Ibn ʿArabī is referring here:

(3) As for 'the knowledge of how to translate from God,' that belongs to every person to whom God speaks through inspiration or by the 'delivery' (to their heart of a particular divine address, *ilqā'*). Because (in such cases) the 'translator' is the one who creates the forms of the spoken or written letters he brings into existence, while the spirit of those forms is God's Speech and nothing else.

And again the sort of 'conclusion' that is a book in itself:

> ...Thus there is nothing in the world but Translator, if it is translated from divine Speaking. So understand!

THE SPIRITUAL QUALITIES OF INSPIRED RIGHT ACTION

Here we can only quote a few highlights of the remaining active, creative qualities of the Mahdi's 'helpers', as Ibn ʿArabī describes them in this chapter 366. Once again, the same rhetorical procedure governs his presentation. At first, the reader's immediate reaction is that Ibn ʿArabī, in describing this 'Mahdi', is only giving the idealised qualities of an almost 'mythical' being, a sort of perfection and purely inspired wisdom that exists only in the tales of the prophets and saints, sometime safely after their death. But then other parts of his description force his reader to begin thinking, at the very least, of the extraordinary range of degrees of approximation to (and distance from) each of these ideal qualities which actually do exist in others we know, and perhaps even in our own experience. (For it is clear that something like this inspired practical wisdom actually does exist, if only from those unforgettable situations—as we have all also experienced—when such 'inspiration' and divine guidance has been so terribly and visibly lacking.) At the next stage, his thoughtful reader necessarily begins to reflect on the possible source and conditions of such inspiration and practical wisdom in each of these domains, especially when and as we actually do begin to discover in ourselves (and simultaneously encounter in others) at least the seeds of each of these essential spiritual qualities:

> (4) As for 'appointing the ranks of the holders of authority', that is the knowledge of what each rank rightfully requires (in order to assure the) kinds of welfare for which it was created. The person possessing this knowledge looks at the soul of the person whom he wants to place in a position of authority and weighs the appropriateness of that person for that rank. If he sees that there is the right equilibrium between the person and the post, without any excess or deficiency, then he gives him that authority... But if the person is inadequate to the position he does not entrust him with that authority, because he

lacks the knowledge that would qualify him for that rank, so that he would inevitably commit injustice…

(5) As for 'mercy in anger,' that is only in the divinely prescribed penalties and punishment, since in everything else (i.e., in merely human judgements) there is anger without any compassion at all…For if a human being gets angry of his own accord, his anger does not contain compassion in any respect. But if someone becomes angry for God's sake, then their anger is God's Anger—and God's Anger is never free from being mixed with divine Compassion. Because (God's) Compassion, since it has precedence over (His) Anger,[88] entirely covers all creatures and *extends to everything* (7:156)…

(6) As for 'the forms of (spiritual) sustenance needed by the ruler,' this (requires) that he know the kinds of worlds, which are only two—i.e., by 'world' I mean the worlds in which this Imam's influence is effective, which are the world of (bodily) forms, and the world of the (human) souls governing those forms with regard to their physical movements and activities…

(7) As for the 'knowledge of the interpenetration of things'[89]…, that (reality) inwardly penetrates and informs all the practical and intellectual crafts. Therefore if the Imam knows this, he will not be bothered by doubt and uncertainty in his judgements. For this (precise inner awareness of the interpenetration of spiritual and manifest reality) is the Scale (of divine justice) in the world, both in sensible things and in the inner spiritual meanings. So the rational, responsible person behaves according to that Scale in both worlds—and indeed in every matter where he has control over his actions.

This section (7) is one of the longest and best-known passages this famous chapter, no doubt because Ibn ʿArabī here so

[88] Alluding to a famous divine saying (*ḥadīth qudsī*) which expresses one of the central themes of all of his writing.

[89] That is, of the penetration of spiritual realities, sources and meanings in everything that we normally or unconsciously take to be 'material', earthly or simply 'natural'.

vehemently and unambiguously contrasts the divinely inspired, personally revealed spiritual knowing of the 'rightly guided one' and these 'Helpers' with the familiar pretensions of the traditionally learned scholars (*'ulamā'*)—and especially with the so-called 'understanding' (*fiqh*) of the jurists of his own time and culture.[90] However, in the context of our discussion here, it is essential above all to grasp that Ibn ʿArabī's fundamental contrast between truly inspired spiritual knowing and our normal—and in many ways unavoidable—reliance on socially and historically constructed forms of belief and persuasion is something essential and inescapably bound up with the human (earthly) condition as such,[91] by no means limited to the particular illustrations and situations he provides from his own culture. Here is a succinct and representative sample of Ibn 'Arabī's quite uncharacteristically direct speech at this point:

> Now the Prophet does exist and is found (here and now) with the People of Unveiling, and therefore they only take their (inspired awareness of the appropriate divine) judgement from him. This is the reason why the truthful and sincere *faqīr*[92] doesn't depend on any (legal) school: he is with the Messenger alone, whom he directly witnesses, just as the Messenger is with the

[90] We have analysed those extremely important passages, in their wider context in the *Futūḥāt* and Islamic thought, in several other essays. See especially the articles cited in notes 65-66 above, and our discussions of the unique role (and rhetorical nature) of Ibn ʿArabī's writings at the end of our article on 'Situating Islamic "Mysticism": Between Written Traditions and Popular Spirituality', in *Mystics of the Book: Themes, Topics and Typologies*, ed. R. Herrera (New York and Berlin, Peter Lang, 1993), pp. 293-334.

[91] This contrast is one of his many distinctive ways of expressing Plato's complex imagery in the Sun-line-Cave section of the *Republic* (whose imagery of course also parallels in fundamental ways the central symbolism of the Qur'an); see the key corresponding image from the *Futūḥāt*, chapter 317, referred to at n. 86 above (article including English translation).

[92] Typically, Ibn 'Arabī here uses this familiar term, ordinarily referring to virtually any Sufi or 'dervish' (the Persian translation of this same Arabic word), in a radically different, ontologically and spiritually precise sense profoundly rooted in the Qur'anic discussions of spiritual 'poverty' (*faqr*) and God's corresponding 'Self-sufficiency' (*ghinā'*). Here the '*faqīr*' is that rare person who has actually realized our absolute and unqualified dependency on God, and thus is in a constant inner state of 'listening' and awaiting what comes from There.

divine inspiration that is sent down to him... But those adhering to knowledge of the external forms (of religious tradition) do not have this (spiritual) rank, because of their having devoted themselves to their love for (prominent social) position, the domination of others, (furthering) their precedence over God's servants and (insuring that) the common people need them. Hence *they do not prosper* (16:116) with regard to their souls, nor shall one prosper spiritually through (following) them... Thus when the rightly-guided one (the 'Mahdi') comes forth (to establish justice in the world) he has no *open enemy* (2:188; etc.) except for the jurists in particular... And as for the person who claims to be divinely informed about the judgements prescribed by the revelation (*shar*ᶜ), for (these jurists), such a person is a madman whose imagination has gone wild, and they would pay no attention to him.

The eighth distinctive spiritual quality of these 'Helpers', their absolute compassion (*raḥma*) and unhindered devotion to the spiritual welfare of all the creatures, is the single theme to which Ibn ᶜArabī devotes perhaps the greatest emphasis throughout all of his writings, above all whenever he is discussing the highest stages of spiritual perfection, the station of the 'solitary ones' (the *afrād*) among the 'Friends of God':

(8) Now as for 'striving to one's utmost and going to any length to satisfy the needs of humanity,' that is especially incumbent upon the Imam in particular, even more than (it is) for the rest of the people. For God only gave him precedence over His (other) creatures and appointed him as their Imam so that he could strive to achieve what is beneficial for them. This striving and what results from it are both prodigious...

(9) As for 'possessing the knowledge of the Unseen that he requires for (rightly governing) this engendered world in particular during a particular period of time,' this is the ninth matter which the Imam requires for his leadership, and there are no (others) besides these...

THE MIRACULOUS PERCEPTION OF BEAUTY (*IḤSĀN*)

Ibn ʿArabī's descriptions of our soul's gradual awakening to the omnipresence of divine inspiration, and to the active responsibilities of creation which flow from that awakening, are intentionally complex, difficult, and challenging. Their meaning and implications only unfold through a long dialectical effort of reflection on their actual—and necessarily unique and individual—reference-points in each person's unfolding experience of transformation. Fortunately, the final section of chapter 366, enumerating a long and fascinating series of descriptions of the distinctive sorts of 'inspired knowing' (*ʿilm*) which are also inherent in this spiritual waystation, gives some powerful hints of how each human being is granted occasional 'tastes' of this reality in ways which then suddenly come to orient our path by so powerfully revealing something of its Goal.

In the famous 'hadith of Gabriel', the actualisation and gradual perfection of Religion, of our human destiny—that is, the earthly realisation of those 'spiritually appropriate actions' of which the Qur'an so constantly speaks—is said to reside in *iḥsān*, literally in '*doing what is both beautiful and good*'. Thus the very possibility of 'making beautiful', as the Prophet's extraordinary reply to Gabriel's question ('What is *iḥsān*?') in that hadith makes very clear, is dependent on our prior spiritual perception and awareness of what is *truly* beautiful and good. *Iḥsān*, Muhammad responds, '*is that you serve-and-worship your God as though you see Him. And even if you don't see Him, He sees you*'. Without any exaggeration, all of Ibn ʿArabī's writing and teaching can be understood as a long running commentary on this teaching. Each person has already been granted, however briefly, some taste of each of these 'openings' Ibn ʿArabī describes here, and such moments of inspired knowing are never forgotten. For each of us, in the long run, that 'tasting' becomes inseparable from the further tasks of insight and creativity it so indelibly reveals:

> ...In this (spiritual stage) there is a knowing which removes the

burden of anguish from the soul of the person who knows it.[93] For when one looks at what is ordinarily the case with (people's) souls, the way that all the things happening to them cause them such anguish and distress, (it is enough) to make a person want to kill himself because of what he sees. This knowing is called the 'knowing of blissful repose', because it is the knowing of the People of the Garden (of Paradise) in particular. So whenever God reveals this knowing to one of the people of this world (already) in this world, that person has received in advance the blissful repose of eternity—although the person with this quality (in this world) still continues to respect the appropriate courtesy[94] (towards God) concerning the commandment of what is right and the prohibition of what is wrong, according to their rank.

And in this stage is the knowing that what God has made manifest to vision in the bodies is an adornment for those bodies; (the knowing) of why it is that some of what is manifest seems ugly to a particular person when they regard it as ugly; and (the knowing) of *which* eye it is that a person sees with when they see the whole world as beautiful, when they do see it, so that they respond to it spontaneously with beautiful actions. Now this knowing is one of the most beautiful (or 'best') and most beneficial forms of knowing about the world…

This stage also includes knowing of what God has placed in the world as (an object for) marvel—and the 'marvellous' (as people usually understand it) is only what breaks with the habitual (course

[93] 'Burden of anguish' translates the Qur'anic term *ḥaraj*, referring here to the inner state of constraint, oppression, anxiety, distress, etc. that usually accompanies and underlies (whether consciously or not) much of our everyday psychic and outward activity. In connection with the subject of this chapter 366 and the special divine inspiration characterising the Mahdi (or his 'Helpers'), a number of Qur'anic verses stress that there is '*no ḥaraj for you in Religion*' (*al-Dīn*; see 22:78; etc.) or in the '*Book sent down*' from God (7:2), and that this familiar state of inner distress is a sign of '*those wandering astray*', while it is removed from those whom God '*guides rightly*' and who inwardly surrender to Him (6:125). It is thus the opposite of *salām* or *taslīm*, 'surrender-to-Peace', and echoes the repeated Qur'anic description of the '*friends of God*' as '*knowing no fear, nor do they sorrow*'.

[94] I.e., *adab*, the proper respect or 'principles of conduct' regarding God in every aspect of one's spiritual life. Its true, inspired and therefore spontaneous expression, as Ibn ʿArabī indicates here and in many other places, obviously varies greatly according to each person's spiritual state and specific conditions.

of things).[95] But for those who comprehend things from the divine perspective, every thing in this 'habitual' course is itself an object of marvel, whereas the 'people of habits' only wonder at what departs from that habitual course.

THE 'LESSER IMAMATE' OR 'VICE-REGENCY' OF EACH HUMAN BEING

After chapter 366, Ibn 'Arabī subsequently mentions the '*mahdī*' only once in passing, but repeatedly returns to the spiritually central question of that 'lesser Imamate' or 'vice-regency' (*al-imāmat al-ṣughrā*, or *al-khilāfat al-ṣughrā*) which is incumbent on each truly human being (*insān*). Each time he amplifies his earlier remarks in new and revealing ways. Thus, soon after this key chapter on 'right guidance', in chapter 370,[96] he discusses this question again in terms clearly evoking his larger understanding of the cosmic spiritual hierarchy:

> The (responsibility of) *khilāfa* (human 'vice-regency' for God) is greater and lesser: for the greatest *khilāfa* is that than which there is no greater, which is the 'greatest Imamate' over the world. The 'lesser Imamate' is (a person's) *khilāfa* over their own self/soul. And as for what is between those two (extremes), that covers everything that is 'lesser' in relation to what lies above it, while it is 'greater' in relation to what is beneath it.

At the beginning of chapter 404,[97] Ibn 'Arabī's explanation is far

[95] *kharq al-ʿāda*: this expression (borrowed from kalam theology, but used here in a radically different, quite concrete spiritual context) is used throughout this section as a sort of pun corresponding to two very different conceptions of the divine 'habit' or 'custom' (*ʿāda*). Ordinarily this term refers to the unenlightened perception of the usual course of affairs in the world, which the 'people of habits' heedlessly take for granted. Hence the usual understanding of *kharq al-ʿāda* as some exceptional 'miracle,' 'prodigy' or 'supernatural' event departing from that unconscious norm. But the true Knowers—those who actually 'see things as they really are'—are profoundly aware of the genuinely miraculous re-creation of the world at every instant, of this ongoing 'marvellous,' never-repeated theophany of Being in *all* Its infinite Self-manifestations.

[96] III, 408, corresponding to the Sura of Abraham (14), a paragon of the status of God's 'Steward' or 'Vice-Regent' (*khalīfa*).

[97] In the following overall Section of the *Futūḥāt*, the *faṣl al-munāzalāt*, vol. IV, 5-6.

more explicit and all-inclusive:

> God said: '*Praise be to God, Lord of the worlds*' (1:2), and He didn't say 'Lord of Himself', because a thing isn't really 'related' to itself. Now this is a divine admonition (*waṣīya*) to His servants, inasmuch as He created them according to His Form,[98] and He gave to those among them to whom He gave it 'the Greater Imamate'[99] and the Imamate of this lower world (*al-dunyā*) and all that lies between them.[100]
>
> So that is (the explanation for) the Prophet's saying: '*Each one of you-all is a shepherd* (or 'guardian', *rāʿī*) *and is responsible for his flock.*' Thus the highest of the shepherds/guardians is the 'greater Imamate,' and the lowest of them is the Imamate of (each) human being over his own actions; and what is between those two includes those who have the Imamate over their family and children and students and possessions.
>
> For there is no human being (*insān*) who was not created according to His Form, and therefore the (responsibility of) the Imamate extends to absolutely all human beings, and that status applies to *every* single (human being) insofar as they are Imam. For what (each human being) possesses[101] is more or less extensive, as we have established. But the Imam is responsible for safeguarding the states of his possessions at every instant. And *this* is the Imam who has truly

[98] Echoing the words of the famous hadith, that 'Adam [or: 'human being', *al-insān*] was created according to the form of *al-rahmān*, '*the All-Loving*'. The most accessible and well-known exposition of this central theme in all of Ibn 'Arabî's works is in the famous opening chapter (on Adam) of his *Fuṣūṣ al-Ḥikam.*

[99] Alluding to the metaphysically fundamental Qur'anic account (at 33:72) of the human being (*insān*) as alone accepting the divine '*Trust*' (*al-amāna*) of the Spirit and the theomorphic totality of the divine Names, rejected by the all the other creatures, including '*the heavens, the earth and the mountains*'. This verse was traditionally viewed as expressing the same reality conveyed in the celebrated divine saying discussed in the previous note.

[100] That is, the *barzakh*, or infinite 'intermediate realm' of the divine creative Imagination, *al-khiyāl*, encompassing all the existent forms of divine Self-manifestation.

[101] Literally, their 'kingdom' or 'property' (*mulk*), a Qur'anic expression normally connected with God—hence a more particular, pointed allusion by Ibn 'Arabī to the actual far-reaching consequences of this intrinsic human responsibility—of all human beings—of 'vice-regency'.

realised the full extent of what God has granted him and entrusted to him.

THE *WILĀYA* (RIGHT RULERSHIP) OF OUR SOULS

Finally, in his vast concluding chapter 560 of 'spiritual advice for both the seeker and for the one who has arrived (with God)',[102] Ibn 'Arabī repeats the same exhortation in terms that are even clearer and more direct—but whose full import can only be evident to someone who has actually read through these 'Illuminations' to this point:

> You should uphold God's 'limits' (*ḥudūd*) with regard to yourself and whatever you possess, for you are responsible to God for that. So if you are a ruler (*sulṭān*), you have been designated for upholding God's limits regarding all He has entrusted to you.
>
> For (according to the hadith) 'each one of you-all is a shepherd, and responsible for his flock', and (that responsibility) is nothing other than upholding God's limits regarding them.
>
> Therefore the lowest form of 'right rulership' (*wilāya*) is your governance of your soul and your actions. So uphold God's limits respecting them until (you reach) the 'greater *Khilāfa*'—for you are God's representative (*nā'ib*) in every situation regarding your own soul and what is above it (i.e., the Spirit).

*

Returning to the mysterious verses that opened this chapter (36:20-21), we are reminded that Sura *Yā Sīn* (36) has traditionally been known as 'the heart of the Qur'an'. As for those who have followed Ibn ʿArabī this far—who have come to recognise, with him, how essential and unavoidable is that ongoing search for true spiritual insight and divinely guided creativity (*iḥṣān*) through which alone we can begin to realize the fully human being (*insān*): such readers may now return to that revelation better prepared to recognize and heed that 'running man', better knowing how to rightly follow every one of 'those who are sent'.

[102] At IV, 462-63; this immense concluding chapter is often popularly reprinted as a large, separate book.

CHAPTER THREE

Ostad Elahi and the Task of Spiritual Intelligence

THOSE WHO ARE familiar with Ibn ʿArabī will certainly recognise many of the same key ideas and guiding intentions, seven centuries later, in the teachings of the recent Iranian thinker, spiritual teacher and musician Ostad Elahi (1895-1974).[103] But the radical contrast in form between the characteristically esoteric, mysteriously symbolic and intentionally veiled language of Ibn ʿArabī's writings, and the directness and simplicity of Ostad Elahi's later oral teachings, is no less striking. Clearly the remarkable differences in the form and expression of those teachings, more than seven centuries later, reflect the radically different circumstances—and corresponding new challenges—of the transformed worlds in which we live today, a point to which we will return in our concluding Postscript below.

THE AUTOBIOGRAPHICAL CONTEXT OF OSTAD ELAHI'S TEACHING

Since the teachings of Ostad Elahi—like those of all great spiritual teachers—are so inseparable from his own life, we must begin by recalling a few basic facts to help situate the context of his teaching and the personal experiences he often used to express his ideas. To begin with, the outward course of Ostad Elahi's biography clearly falls into three distinct periods. For the first twenty-five years of his life, he led an ascetic, secluded life of rigorous spiritual discipline under his father's careful guidance, a life completely devoted to the forms of contemplation and the classical religious studies (in Persian, Arabic and Kurdish) developed over centuries of mystical tradition in his homeland. Some time after his father's death in 1920,

[103] See now Jean During's magisterial study *L'âme des sons: L'art unique d'Ostad Elahi (1895-1974)*, Gordes, le Relié, 2001; an English translation is in preparation.

however, Ostad Elahi eventually left his traditional contemplative life for a much more active career as a magistrate and judge, a radical change that was necessary to broaden his experience and to test and prove his ethical and religious principles in the crucible of all the challenges of an active social and professional life 'in the world'. As he himself later described it,

> God made me enter the public administration and government work despite my own aversion for that. He made me a judge by force and gave me difficult judicial assignments. But afterwards I discovered that in each of these posts were concealed thousands of nuggets of wisdom, such that even a multitude of philosophers and sages gathered together couldn't have designed such plans...[104]

Thus it was only after his retirement from public service in 1957 that Ostad Elahi actually published his written works and began to be approached by seekers from all walks of life and from the most diverse religious and national backgrounds, who came to visit him and pose their questions at his home in Tehran. Our focus here is on the personal, oral spiritual teaching which unfolded in that informal setting, since it is most universal and widely accessible in its form of expression. Once one is familiar with the broader, more universal expression of Ostad Elahi's thought in the oral teachings discussed here, it will become clear that each of his other books is basically a thorough explanation of those same spiritual principles for different traditional learned audiences.[105]

Although focusing (as the title indicates) on the nature, context and influences of Ostad Elahi's extraordinary musical work, the vast majority of During's insights and observations are directly relevant to the spoken (and written) forms of his spiritual teaching discussed in this chapter. (See other biographical studies, translations, etc. in Further Reading below.)

[104] AH 1966. All sayings quoted below are from the two published volumes of transcriptions of Ostad Elahi's oral teachings (in Persian, with some Arabic and Kurdish) during the last years of his life, *Āthār al-Ḥaqq* ('*Traces of the Truth*'): see publication details in Further Reading below. *AH* = volume I, followed by the particular number of the 2082 sayings in that volume (numbered consecutively through all 24 chapters; those numbers are *not* dates). *R* = chapter and selection number from an as yet unpublished French anthology [*Recueil*] of O. Elahi's sayings, ed. B. Elahi, also primarily drawn from the two volumes of *Āthār al-Ḥaqq*.

[105] See Further Reading below for details on forthcoming publication of our translation and study of his '*Knowing the Spirit*', and planned translations of his

Ostad Elahi's more informal and personal, oral teachings, which were set forth in discussions and explanations for people of all ages and backgrounds who came to him for guidance during the last years of his life, were carefully recorded and transcribed by a number of his close students. To date, two massive Persian collections of those sayings—together the equivalent of a dozen or more volumes in translation—have been published, and all the passages quoted here are drawn from those two published collections. The fact that these were originally oral teachings does not at all mean that they are somehow 'minor' or unsystematic, in comparison with his above-mentioned writings. In fact, as those familiar with Sufism and other spiritual traditions well know, the directly open, spontaneous and less symbolic expression of many of the most central spiritual teachings have often been reserved for an intimate circle of trusted disciples.[106] And in any event, many of Ostad Elahi's own remarks make it clear that he was also aware of the lasting importance of his spoken words.

SPIRITUAL PRACTICE AND COMMUNICATION

Before describing some of the key systematic principles of Ostad Elahi's spiritual teaching, though, it is helpful to highlight something of the essential characteristics of the very form and expression of that teaching. Not only does this help convey some of the distinctive flavour and humanity of his personality, but these particular sayings also contain important practical lessons for our own tasks of spiritual learning and communication.

First of all, Ostad Elahi's teaching is typically based directly on his own lifelong personal experience and 'testing' of his principles, often expressed in openly autobiographical anecdotes and stories. As he once put it,

---

other written works, which developed many of the same spiritual insights and teachings summarised here, but in the complex idiom of classical theological and philosophic learning familiar to the learned Iranian public of that time—a philosophical language itself still very strongly influenced (via the 17th-century philosopher Mullā Ṣadrā) by the ideas and approaches of Ibn 'Arabî.

[106] This is clearly the case, for example, with many of the fundamental topics discussed in Ostad Elahi's *Knowing the Spirit* (*Maʿrifat ar-Rūḥ*): see Further Reading below for our forthcoming translation.

> When I tell you all these things my purpose is not just to recount stories, but to pass on spiritual wisdom. I'm not able to advise anyone about something until I've put it into practice for myself. I don't mention anything that I haven't explored completely. I have not imitated anyone: my ideas are the result of my own discoveries and my own personal experiences. I have summarised the very essence of the foundation of all the true religions in these few words that I've left for those travelling the path of God. Throughout my life, whenever I didn't know something I've never been ashamed to say so. And I've always tried to speak truthfully and precisely.[107]

Or expressed as a more general principle, which anyone can readily test in their own life:

> Every word that comes from lived experience and personal observation has an immediate spiritual influence.[108]

Secondly, if the outward form of Ostad Elahi's teaching is often apparently simple, such as recounting a dream or an outwardly mundane personal experience, that reflects his constant stress on the fact that the process of spiritual teaching and learning, for each one of us, necessarily takes place through our reflection on the deeper meaning and challenges of spiritual lessons grounded in and emerging naturally from the ongoing context of each person's everyday life:

> It is in everyday life that I've learned the most lessons about the underlying order of the universe. This world becomes a place for spiritual edification once we discover how to draw those lessons from it—even from the flight of a mosquito.[109]

> And 'The person who in their everyday life draws conclusions on the basis of little things will always succeed in life; while on the contrary, someone who tries to draw particular conclusions from generalities will not succeed in life.'

[107] *R*5-12.
[108] *AH*570.
[109] *R*5-11.

In fact, the deeper reality evoked in such outwardly simple stories and sayings is often inexhaustible, and those same spiritual laws and regularities will continue to be understood and realised in new ways at each of the ascending levels of spiritual practice and realisation:

> The revelations of the spiritual world are like a fruit that one opens and discovers within it ten seeds; then within each of those seeds are ten seeds, and within each one of those ten more, and so on to infinity.[110]

Finally, the implication of this constant focus on the spiritual lessons to be found in all aspects of life is that the 'truth' intended for each person can only be found and fully realised through our own individual spiritual practice, included the essential process of reflection and spiritual intelligence integrally grounded in practice, not simply through the intellectual elaboration of a special 'theory' or particular system of ideas or beliefs:

> Everything that has marked a person's heart and faith has a spiritual effect, however they may speak about it. Forget about fancy words, faith is what matters—I mean, what has an effect is that in which we have faith and which we put into practice. When we ourselves have put something into practice and speak about that, our words have an effect. But if we don't practice it, then there's no use in talking about it and developing proofs and arguments—none of that will have any effect. Because when we practice something, we don't even need to talk about it: our actions and behaviour will have an effect all by themselves.[111]

This is certainly *not* to say that reflection and understanding are not also essential to the task of spiritual learning, but rather that they must always be firmly grounded in practice and real experience. For then, as he memorably points out:

> The person who has (spiritual) knowledge and puts their faith into practice is like someone who completes their (spiritual) journey by

[110] *AH* 657.
[111] *AH* 660.

> airplane. The person who practices religion without understanding is like someone who makes the same journey very slowly, as though travelling by donkey. But someone who has such knowledge and fails to put it into practice is even worse off than the person who is practising it without any knowledge.[112]

All this is only an application of the deeper metaphysical principle, however apparently simple, that 'The Real [or 'True Reality': *al-Ḥaqq*] has no need of proofs and arguments. It is Its own proof.' That is a helpful caution to keep in mind as we turn to some of the key systematic features of Ostad Elahi's teaching.

THE PROCESS OF SPIRITUAL PERFECTION

Perhaps nothing more readily sums up Ostad Elahi's teaching than to say it is about the soul's quest for the Truth (or 'the Real': *al-Ḥaqq*): all the metaphysical, theological, and practical spiritual themes that he develops in response to his interlocutors' questions revolve around this central idea. And that quest, as he so often reiterates, comes down to three equally essential questions:

> Truth (or 'the Real'), for every human being, consists in knowing who we are: (that is to say) where we have come from, what we must do, and where we should be going... When that search has become the guiding principle for our actions, when we have put it into practice and discovered the answers: then we have reached the Truth/the Real (*Ḥaqq*).[113]
>
> And 'The essence of real spiritual knowledge is when you understand why you have come into existence, what are your duties in that existence, and what is your ultimate goal... Our goal should be to act in accordance with the divine principles in order to reach perfection...'[114]

While the answers to all three of these basic metaphysical questions can be developed to infinity—and do in fact receive detailed

[112] *R*1-11.
[113] *R*1- 2.
[114] *R*1-3.

and systematic treatment in each of Ostad Elahi's own writings[115] as well as his oral teachings—it is characteristic of the practical focus of his spiritual teaching that what is most essential and immediate, once we have acquired a basic awareness of where we have come from and where we are ultimately going, is the focus on what we should be doing here and now, in this world and this life:

> If a person truly understands, through their faith and inner certainty, these three principles: that there is One God, that the soul lives on, and that there is another accounting and record (of our life) than what we can see in this world—then that is sufficient for them.[116]

In the remainder of this discussion, we shall have to assume the wider metaphysical, theological and eschatological framework of Ostad Elahi's thought, which is systematically developed at great length in both his written and oral teachings, and focus here on certain key features of his understanding of our spiritual situation and our essential practical duties. So we may begin by outlining, as concisely as possible, his understanding of the nature of the human soul or 'self', in both its spiritual and animal dimensions, and of the path of gradual perfection that naturally leads from inner knowledge of the soul to the unfolding of true knowledge of God and eventually to the highest stages of spiritual perfection. Then we shall turn to—and conclude with—key aspects of his practical ethical teaching concerning the actual *work* of perfection, the complex of responsibilities and virtues that together can move us through this path of realisation.

SOUL, SPIRIT AND DIMENSIONS OF THE 'SELF'

Ostad Elahi constantly reminds us that our human situation, while it carries unique spiritual responsibilities and challenges, is necessarily part of a much larger, truly universal process of perfection:

> The process of perfection that passes from the mineral to the

[115] In particular, all of Ostad Elahi's *Knowing the Spirit* (see Further Reading below and our forthcoming English translation) is entirely devoted to elaborating that larger context.

[116] *AH* 665.

> vegetal state, from the vegetal to the animal, and from the animal to the human state is a natural and predetermined movement. The minerals, plants and animals don't have the power of reason, and their development takes place...in a way that is natural and automatic. But the process of perfection in human beings takes place according to a different set of rules, since we have an angelic soul. Each human being is endowed with reason, and it is through our own efforts that we can eventually reach perfection... [117]

For Ostad Elahi, therefore, the embodied human soul, or 'self', is the unique combination and meeting-point of two very different dimensions: first, of the individual 'angelic soul', or immortal human spirit (*rūḥ*), which is derived from the divine 'Breath' and always remains directly connected to God—even if we are not usually aware of that inner connection; and secondly, of a specific mortal, 'human-animal' ('basharic') soul,[118] which is itself a uniquely individual combination of earlier animal, vegetal and mineral souls now connected to this particular human body. (For the sake of brevity, we may refer to this mortal, basharic soul by the familiar Perso-Arabic expression, the *nafs*.) For Ostad Elahi, the connection and combination of these two dimensions of our soul and self is not some sort of 'trap' or 'prison' to be escaped. Instead, as we shall see, it is precisely their complex combination that creates the unique earthly situation through which the angelic soul or spirit is gradually able to learn and develop to its full spiritual potential. As he summarises it,

> ...The mineral, vegetal, animal and basharic souls are all material (and therefore mortal); only the angelic soul or 'spirit' can be included among the incorporeal beings. When a person dies, it is the angelic soul that carries away with it the lasting impressions of those four (material) souls.[119]

[117] *R*3-5.

[118] The terminology reflects the same fundamental Qur'anic contrast of the theomorphic, 'fully human' *insān*, and the complex mortal biped (*bashar*), which likewise structured the essential philosophic and spiritual teachings of both our earlier thinkers.

[119] *AH*811 (and *AH*806).

For this reason, Ostad Elahi always insists that the way back to a true realisation of our own spiritual nature and relation to God—and ultimately to all the spiritual worlds and realms of Perfection—necessarily begins through seeking and developing a deeper awareness of our soul and our true spiritual self. Or in other words,

> The spirit (or 'angelic soul', the *rūḥ*) is the true being, and the body is only the instrument of that being, not the true being itself. Whoever reaches the final stage of Perfection enters the ocean of the Unicity of Being—but each particle (of that Being) conserves its own individuality.[120]

Of course, saying this is one thing, and actually doing it—as we all know—is quite another. So before going on to quote more of Ostad Elahi's teaching concerning this unfolding path through self-knowledge to deeper knowledge of God and the corresponding awareness of those responsibilities[121] that eventually lead to Perfection, it is essential to explain what might at first look like a strange paradox between this broad metaphysical outlook and his practical ethical and spiritual teaching. Why, as we shall see, does Ostad Elahi go on to insist that an active, responsible social life of involvement in this world is so absolutely essential to our process of self knowledge? The key lies in this short and simple saying:

> No creature is completely immobile; they are all constantly in movement—only in a 'trans-substantial movement.' [122] This universal trans-substantial motion exists in all beings and animates the entire universe. This movement is caused by the absolute movement of the divine Essence to which each being is directly connected. This is the phenomenon that they call the 'immediate connection' between God and each of the creatures, which explains how God is

[120] *AH* 789.

[121] And 'rights'—of God, the spirit, and all other creatures: see the Introduction above for these other, equally indispensable dimensions of the divine *Ḥaqq*.

[122] The underlying technical term here is the famous *ḥaraka jawharīya*, drawn from its central usage in the philosophy of Mullā Ṣadrā (who in turn adapted this key teaching from Ibn 'Arabī). Much of Ostad Elahi's *Knowing the Spirit* (see Further Reading below for our forthcoming translation and study of this key work) is devoted to a detailed discussion and explanation of this cosmological and ontological principle of all creation.

omnipresent in all creation. There is also an indirect connection (between God and the creatures), based on the laws of cause and effect. This universal, trans-substantial movement exists in minerals, plants, animals, and in general in every creature.[123]

SELF-KNOWLEDGE AND THE PATH OF SPIRITUAL PERFECTION

For Ostad Elahi—whose entire perspective can be seen as an explanation of the famous dictum (often transmitted as a Prophetic hadith) 'Whoever knows their self/soul, knows their Lord'—the human starting point of the process of spiritual perfection is always each individual's gradually unfolding awareness of their true self, of the 'Heart' (*qalb/dil*):

> Everyone sees the external world through the prism of their own heart. What we see is the image of what is in our heart reflected in the world outside us.[124]

In other words, we can only begin to know the many dimensions and depths of our true self—and to polish the mirror of our heart—through the conflicts and challenges of our social and ethical life in the world with others. Or as he puts it in another equally succinct saying:

> As long as we have not polished our own heart like a mirror, we cannot see God. For God isn't separate from us, and turning this way or that won't help (to find Him). Thus the knowledge of our duty becomes our knowledge of God.[125]

At this point, we can simply quote a long saying that summarises in more detail—but still in abstract outline form—the successive stages in this unfolding process of spiritual awareness:

Reaching the spiritual stage of 'knowing one's self' is an essential precondition for beginning the stage of 'coming to know God'... In other words, the knowledge of God we're referring to here means coming to know God within our self, and these two stages both lead up to the stage of the soul's journey toward spiritual perfection.[126]

[123] *R*3-9.
[124] *R*2-13.
[125] *AH*735.
[126] *R*2-3.

...When a person reflects deeply on their origin, their ultimate goal, and the reasons why they are here in this world, that is the stage of coming to know one's self. The fundamental condition for reaching this knowledge of our self is to become a true, fully human being—which means to want for others what we want for ourself. Putting that principle into practice leads such a person to the point where all the essential qualities of true humanity automatically emanate from them.

After the spiritual stage of knowing one's self, a person necessarily begins to ask where we have come from and who created us. This is the question that makes us begin to turn our attention toward the Creator, and that is how we set out on the stage of coming to know God. Through reasoning, a person can understand that we didn't create ourselves and that we weren't created by others like us, but by a creator who is superior to us. As we go farther, it becomes clear that we cannot pursue forever this chain of 'who created whom,' and that this original Creator is therefore necessarily both unique and existing for all eternity.

Once we have reached this conclusion, we begin to ask where it is we must seek this Creator. And ...as we delve within our self, we can see all the traces and impressions within us that bear witness to our Creator. Then eventually, in that state of union and ecstasy, we are able to contemplate God's reflection and manifestation within our own being...And the key of knowledge of God reveals everything that is necessary to us along the spiritual path and shows us how it is useful. From then on we are truly 'on track' and know what we need to understand. Once we understand that the source of our knowledge of our self and our knowledge of God is one and the same, then we have begun the stage of the journey toward spiritual perfection.

Translating this road-map into the actual journey, of course, is something else. And the decisive practical importance of right action and attentiveness toward God in undertaking that journey is well summed up in another memorable saying:

The impression of everything that has ever been created in the universe lies within each human being. If we delve within our self and focus our attention, we can come to discern all sorts of inexplicable things and resolve a great many mysteries, thanks to that power which God has placed within our being…

Once we succeed in delving within our self, everything is unveiled and revealed to us. It may happen that a person is walking along normally, when suddenly they enter into a state of spiritual contemplation. Their heart is connected with the Source, and as a result of that connection they understand everything they need to understand… Yet that same person could pray constantly day and night, and without that inner connection between their heart and the Source they would not discover anything.

In order to find that connection, we must always have our attention focused on God, to such an extent that we spontaneously do what is good and avoid doing anything evil. Really putting these two principles into practice is the key to all those spiritual discoveries and intuitions that will gradually come to guide us later on.[127]

Of course we can hardly begin to undertake any journey without some notion of our goal. The following saying of Ostad Elahi beautifully summarises the inner relations between that spiritual goal and the ongoing concrete, practical facets of our ethical and spiritual existence that actually constitute 'our' own intentional, active contribution to this spiritual journey:

The more a person manages to overcome the desires and passions of their human-animal self (*nafs*), and the closer they come to the stages and sentiments of true humanity and our full human dignity, the more 'perfect' they become… In order for a person to become a fully human being, there are many conditions they must fulfil. It's easy to state these in theory, but the conditions themselves are extremely difficult. The 'perfect human being' is the person who treats everyone else the same way they would like to be treated, and who also defends others against whatever that person would not like for himself. That's easy to say, but very difficult to put into practice. Yet the more you actually apply it in your life, the closer you come to real human being. You have to watch and control yourself at every instant, day and night, and become your own judge.[128]

[127] *R*2-2.
[128] *AH*885.

THE GOAL AND STARTING POINTS: COMPASSION, FAITH, AND THE ROLES OF RELIGION

There are a number of other, even more concise sayings in which Ostad Elahi summarises that spiritual goal in equally visible and practical—and equally difficult—terms. Here are a few of them:

> A true human being is someone who is pleased at the happiness of others and who has sincere compassion for their suffering.[129]
>
> The key to life in this world is respecting the rights of others.[130]
>
> The voyager on the spiritual Path must always preserve the proper equilibrium in each of these four areas: the proper balance between their angelic soul, body, family, and society.[131]

Working toward this goal, however one describes it, is so difficult that dejection and disappointment, even despair, are frequent dangers. Thus, before turning to some of Ostad Elahi's key practical prescriptions for those travelling this Path, it may be helpful to keep in mind what he says about the constant importance of faith, spiritual self-confidence, and self-mastery:

> Everyone's life has its ups and downs. We must try to acquire self-mastery. When a person has become master of their inner states, everything becomes easy. We mustn't 'endure' our destiny, but rather we must take it in hand: in light of our relation to God and His providential caring, we should be so confident and so detached from everything that the decrees of destiny seem insignificant. We shouldn't let upsets and disturbances dominate us: the more we are able to resist being controlled by them, the better we will master the situations we do encounter.[132]
>
> In order to strengthen your self-confidence, the best way is not to focus on your failures, and to continue to pursue your goal as though you hadn't undergone a defeat or failure. The secret of the success of all great human beings comes from that attitude.[133]

[129] *R*4-6.
[130] *R*4-7.
[131] *R*4-20.
[132] *R*4-9.
[133] *AH*595.

Now throughout human history, one of the most essential, indispensable guides to this process of spiritual perfection, in all of its dimensions, has of course been that complex reality we call Religion.[134] Not surprisingly, much of Ostad Elahi's practical teaching—like that of every great spiritual guide and teacher—was constantly focused on clarifying the proper relations between the different dimensions and functions of religions, especially as they contribute to the realisation of our ultimate spiritual end.

Perhaps the best way to approach this subject, once again, is to begin by evoking the ultimate human goal, the reality of being and truth as witnessed by the fully human being. That condition is beautifully summarised in Ostad Elahi's response to the naive question: 'What is the meaning of true spiritual understanding (*ᶜirfān*)?':

> When you realise that every person you happen to see is a 'spiritual knower' (*ᶜārif*), then you will have understood the meaning of this. When you've come to see all of the prophets and saints as true, and you no longer distinguish between the different religions, only then you will have reached the stage of true spiritual understanding.[135]

Or even more simply:

> The religion of the Real/the Truth (*al-Ḥaqq*) is One...and all the religions (and prophets) have said it: that you should love and do for others what you wish for yourself...That is the ultimate principle of religion.[136]

In his more theoretical discussions of this question, especially when visitors would seek to compare or criticise different historical religions or particular schools and approaches, Ostad Elahi always began by distinguishing between the unifying, perennial spiritual core and goal shared by all the revealed religions, and the diverse 'exoteric' social, ritual and legal dimensions comprised within each of those historical traditions. For example,

> ...The basis of the revelation [of the common spiritual aim and

[134] Always in the Qur'anic sense of the *divine*, universal reality of *Dīn*.
[135] *R*1-4.
[136] *AH*612.

related prescriptions] is the same for all the religions, and they only differ concerning the unavoidable matters connected with social life. But what is the real, genuine prescription for purification of the soul and ethical perfection is identical in all the (true) religions.[137]

Of course the practical elaboration and clarification of these distinctions is not always an easy matter, and much of Ostad Elahi's work of practical spiritual guidance was devoted to helping students with that unavoidable task of developing appropriate spiritual discernment and practical intelligence. But his most general practical conclusion is well summarised in the following advice:

> The condition of (true) religious life for every human being is, first, to respect all (the true) religions, without rejecting others (than your own); and secondly, whatever the religion you choose, to put it into practice, not just (believing its) words. Because what God is concerned with is our heart and our deeds...[138]

In his own practical teaching and guidance, Ostad Elahi always sought to bring his students back to the spiritual essentials, to making the inner connection between their own religious practice and its ultimate spiritual aim in the purification and perfection of the soul. Some of the most central common practical spiritual teachings shared by all the religions are aptly summarised in the following saying:

> The principles of the (true) religions are all based on certain unshakeable foundations, including inner self-restraint; charity; prayer and invocation; and purity of intention and sincerity toward God...[139]

After describing the fundamental practical role of self-restraint and true charity, he goes on to explain that:

> With prayer and invocations, the essential condition is to focus one's attention on the divine Source, not simply to repeat certain phrases or other ritual prescriptions. And true invocations are when

[137] *AH* 722.
[138] *AH* 718.
[139] *AH* 611.

we truly remember God and our true selves, so as to avoid heedlessness... Purity of intention and sincerity toward God, in practical terms, means that we should want for all creatures those benefits we want for ourself, and that we should not wish for others what we don't want for ourself.

When a person truly practices those four basic principles, then they will be purified and move from their animal state to that of a true, fully human being (*insān*)... In a word, when a person actually becomes truly 'human', their natural inclination always prompts them to act for what is good and right.

ETHICAL AND SOCIAL LIFE IN THE AWAKENING OF SPIRITUAL INTELLIGENCE

One of the most characteristic features of Ostad Elahi's own teaching is his constant insistence on the practical spiritual importance of an active, engaged social life in the world as the most fruitful and productive 'school' for discovering and purifying the inner realities of the soul. As we have already seen, his insistence on this point is surely not unrelated to the dramatic contrast in his own life between his youthful life and training in longstanding traditional forms of contemplative spiritual retreat, and the more complex challenges of his later active professional and teaching career. The ongoing temptations for many of us (particularly in times of difficulty) of a utopian mystical 'retreat' from this world—and the dangerous spiritual pitfalls such temptations necessarily involve—are well illustrated in one of Ostad Elahi's memorable autobiographical anecdotes, where he tells how— 'One night a state of spiritual enthusiasm came over me, and I decided to spend the night alone in prayer and contemplation.'

Then he goes on to describe in humorous terms how noisy neighbours and other distractions forced him up to his roof, out into the streets of Shiraz, and eventually to a remote shrine, without ever finding the quiet he was seeking. Finally, he explains:

During the time I was an investigative magistrate in Shiraz I had rented rooms in a house partly occupied by the owner. The owner of

> the house had many guests that night, and it was very noisy. I shut the doors and opened my window on the street, but there were two porters just outside beneath the window, who were busy discussing their problems. So I closed the window and went up on the roof, but there were already two women up there talking. I had to climb down and went off to Bābā Kūhī [a nearby religious shrine]. Darvīsh ʿAlī, the guardian of that holy place, was an upright and respected ascetic. I asked if I could go into his room to concentrate on my prayers and contemplation, and that he let no one disturb my devotions, and he accepted. So I had entered his room and was just beginning to focus on my spiritual state, when two young women came up and began to talk loudly with Darvish Ali, who was more than a hundred years old. Then I was really at the end of my rope. I came out of the room and asked them to leave him alone, but it turned out they wanted to chat with me too!
>
> In short, that special spiritual state of mine disappeared that night, and no matter what I tried I wasn't really able to meditate. 'O Lord,' I said, 'so You're still testing me? Well then, it's up to You. Thy will be done!' At just that moment a 'voice' responded: 'You must seek that spiritual solitude within your own heart. No place is ever unoccupied; only your heart is free and alone.' Then I understood that they wanted to keep me from secluding myself too much, because recently I'd been a little too withdrawn..., whereas because of my profession I ought to be participating more in social occasions and accepting invitations to be with people. It's not proper to live in seclusion from society. Instead you must live in society while still staying true to your self. Those who choose to isolate themselves in order to avoid the temptations and tests that necessarily come from participating in society, while saying that they are being virtuous, are mistaken. What really counts is to stay in the world and participate in social life while still remaining virtuous and moral.[140]

The deeper reasons why active life in this world is so conducive to attaining greater knowledge of our true self—and ultimately of God and our deeper spiritual duties—become quite clear when we

140 *AH*1924.

consider the basic principles underlying Ostad Elahi's constantly repeated practical advice to those setting out on this Path. Those basic practical principles of right action, from the point of view of attaining those spiritual goals described above, come down to several essential points. First, seeing, saying and wanting what is good, or purifying our moral intentions. Second, struggling against the hidden and visible constraints and limitations of our human-animal self (the *nafs*). Third, constantly focusing our attention on God. And finally, the constant practical necessity of spiritual courage and perseverance (*ṣabr*). Of course in reality—even though here we must outline each of these points in succession—they are each inseparable aspects of the same ongoing practical 'work', the same gradual process of spiritual perfection, and working consciously on any one of these elements inevitably brings into relief the integral role of all the others as well.

In particular, the way each of these three essential aspects of conscious spiritual work leads concretely to greater self-knowledge and increasingly higher levels of spiritual awareness and clarity is well summarised in the following saying:

> ...The (spiritual) cause of whatever happens to us is within ourselves and not outside our self. Therefore we must always search for that cause within our self. Because the further we delve within ourselves, the clearer things become. (For example,) if someone commits a transgression and then things happen to them, that is the consequence of their transgression, since there is no action that does not have a corresponding reaction... So if we take as our religious watchword and precepts what has been taught by the great religious figures, and if we put that into practice with real faith, that will guide us along the right path...[141]

It should not be necessary to explain here how each of these basic practical spiritual principles is expressed in the central teachings of each revealed religious tradition.

[141] *AH* 620.

PURIFICATION OF INTENTION

One key lesson quickly becomes apparent when we begin to practice mindfulness of our ethical motivations, and as we reflect more deeply on the lasting consequences of our actions. That is the central importance of purifying our intention, of always acting from a selfless awareness of what is right and good. There are few aspects of spiritual practice that Ostad Elahi mentions more repeatedly and insistently. Like the other spiritual principles discussed below, this one is easy to put in words, but constantly challenging to put into practice. Yet the spiritual discernment required to distinguish the motives and influences of our human-animal self from genuine spiritual inspiration and truly disinterested (divine) motivation begins already with the most elementary ethical conflicts and trials. Only through the ongoing practice and discovery of this principle can we eventually reach the profound simplicity and humility of the highest degrees of spiritual realisation:

> For when we only desire what pleases God, it's absolutely certain that He won't allow us to be troubled in this world either. But if we want only the things of this world from God we're behaving like a little child who has been given all his fortune and who runs off to buy a lot of candy and eat it all up: he only makes himself sick and afterward there's nothing left for him at all.[142]

One practical expression of this focus on intention, to which Ostad Elahi constantly returns, is the necessity of gradually coming to say and want what is good for everyone—and ultimately even to see everything as good.

> Those who consider themselves voyagers on the spiritual Path should adopt these three principles:
>
> —'To say what is good': this means not to gossip or put down others, not to swear and curse, and so on
>
> —'To see what is good': this means not seeing anything or anyone as evil in themselves, but rather to see the good in every thing…
>
> —'To want and think what is good': this means that whatever we

[142] *AH* 2015.

> want for ourselves, we should also want it for everyone; and it means not to feel hatred, jealousy and bitterness, not to think of getting vengeance, and so on.[143]

Again, it is crucially important to keep in mind that the perception of what is truly 'good' here must be taken in a profoundly spiritual sense—ultimately inseparable from the even more fundamental task of attention to God, to which we will turn in a moment. The 'good' in each of these domains cannot be effortlessly taken from some external source (be it social, cultural, familial, etc.), but can ultimately only be discerned and discovered through the long process of spiritual work itself, as the following saying makes clear:

> To see what is good, think what is good, and say what is good all have an effect whose benefit can be felt by the person who actually practices those principles. That person's heart becomes illuminated, so that they are able to see with full clarity, rather than through the fog of bitterness and resentment.[144]

This basic principle, so often reiterated by every prophet, saint and true spiritual guide, may sound simple in itself, but even the slightest attempt to put it into practice immediately brings us face to face with the next central theme of Ostad Elahi's spiritual teaching, the long and difficult struggle between our spirit (or 'angelic soul') and the human-animal self, the *nafs*, with its endless disguises and ruses.

THE 'SELF' AND SPIRITUAL DISCERNMENT: MINDFULNESS AND SELF-DISCIPLINE

Nothing in human experience could be more absolutely universal—and practically inescapable—than the ongoing inner tension and conflict between the multiple demands, inclinations and tendencies of our specific human-animal nature (the '*nafs*' or basharic self), on the one hand, and our immediate inspired awareness of what is right and our duty in a given situation. As Ostad Elahi puts it,

143 *R*4-12.
144 *R*4-13.

> Our contact with the Source of spiritual realities is what transforms mere animal awareness into a fully human conscience: the result of that contact is that in everything a person undertakes they are immediately inspired as to whether that action is good or bad. Now true conscience/consciousness is precisely that discovery of and penetration into this mystery.[145]

From this perspective, our ethical experience is by its very nature an experience of the divine, and those recurrent situations of outer and inner conflict (the 'tests', in Qur'anic terms) that mark out our life on earth are the essential seedbed for all spiritual growth. By awakening our conscience—that mysterious inner awareness of the divine—those challenging situations are the ever-renewed context of that natural, universal process of spiritual learning and growth which already grounds and structures our human situation. Our essential human task is to begin to participate more and more consciously in that process of spiritual perfection, at increasingly more challenging levels of responsibility.

The basic elements of this situation are extremely simple when expressed in their most abstract form (even if their particular realities are infinitely varied): once we become aware of the initial, essential contrast between the expressions of our animal nature and our truly spiritual and ethical inspiration, the essential spiritual task of each human being is constant 'mindfulness' (*tawajjuh*) or awareness of those divine inspirations, and then the ongoing demands of self-discipline required to translate that mindfulness into the appropriate ethical action, in every inner and outer domain where such challenges arise.

Even at the end of his life, Ostad Elahi could be quite humorous in pointing out the familiarity and omnipresence of this basic human situation:

> Last night I woke up at midnight as usual for my nightly prayers and devotions. But because I was feeling slightly ill, I acted a bit lazy and said to myself: 'I'll pray tomorrow morning', and I went back to sleep. Of course the next morning I performed my prayers, and then I

[145] *AH* 2018.

began to do my exercises. Now I had never dropped one of the exercise weights before, but one of them slipped out of my hand and fell right on my toes. It hurt for an hour. God had reprimanded me to exactly the same extent as I'd been lazy with him—there was something almost comical about it! I was extremely happy about that incident, and I bowed down to God in gratitude on the spot. 'Now I know that You love me', I told Him, 'and that You're always watching over me'.[146]

As this story indicates, one important and recurrent aspect of this constant spiritual struggle is the providential way in which it is precisely our persistent failures and weaknesses that keep each human being constantly in a state of humility and search for divine grace and guidance:

> Each person, in relation to God, should always be in a state of humility, submission and inner surrender to God. That is to say, we should always despair of relying on our own actions, while we should always have hope in God's Grace. The higher a person rises, the greater and weightier their responsibilities become...[147]

Ultimately, even the highest human degrees of awareness of God have their roots in this absolutely universal, intimately familiar situation of inner ethical conflict and the spiritual mindfulness to which it gives rise, when we respond appropriately. Thus Ostad Elahi often emphasises that this ongoing process of ethical struggle and conflict involves coming to know intimately and recognize the presence and workings of each of the three dimensions or manifestations of our angelic soul:[148]

> The 'inspiring soul', which gives us spiritual inspiration; the 'blaming soul', or conscience which reproaches us for each wrong action; and the 'reassuring soul', which gives faith and certitude and reassurance to the true worshipper/ servant of God...[149]

[146] *AH* 2002.
[147] *AH* 836.
[148] The underlying Qur'anic expressions here (*al-nafs al-mulhima*, *al-nafs al-lawwāma*, and *al-nafs al-muṭma'inna*) are of course drawn from the classical Qur'anic vocabulary of Islamic spirituality.
[149] *AH* 824.

Each of the subsequent points outlined below are simply the further consequences of these two fundamental ethico-spiritual tasks of mindfulness and self-discipline. Those further facets of the natural unfolding of each person's process of growth and spiritual perfection are as follows: the centrality of spiritual attention (*tawajjuh*); our observation and reflection on the laws of spiritual causality; the unfolding demands of creativity and responsibility; and the ongoing challenge of perseverance.

ATTENTION TO THE SOURCE

This aspect of Ostad Elahi's practical spiritual teaching is so absolutely fundamental—since it is at once both the goal and the primordial foundation and presupposition of all spiritual work—that even mentioning it sounds like a truism. That most essential point of all is 'attention—and intention—toward God'. And of course it is present at the core of every stage of our religious and spiritual life, as he constantly reminds us. To begin with, in every religion,

> All prayers, invocations and all the rest—(the aim of) all of these can be summed up as maintaining that state of continual attention on God, and trying to learn what we must do in order to please God.[150]
>
> For the very principle of prayer is purpose and intention. Whatever the religion or form of worship, to have your attention on God, to whatever degree, is accepted—whatever the words may be.[151]

But if attention toward God is already central at even the most elementary and external forms of religious life, how much more essential and active it must become as the soul moves, through this spiritual work, along the path of self-knowledge leading to ever deeper and more operative direct awareness of God. The absolute importance of spiritual attentiveness and concentration at these higher stages of the path is beautifully summarised in a passage which also draws together virtually all the points of Ostad Elahi's teaching we have already discussed:

> Following the path of spiritual perfection necessarily requires a

[150] *AH* 659.
[151] *AH* 701.

connection (with God), and that spiritual rank cannot be acquired through artificial methods... Eventually each person must experience for themselves a state of illumination; then through that illumination they will grasp the manifestation of the Truth/the Real.[152]

That (higher spiritual) world is not concerned with the body, but with the angelic soul. So we must orient our soul toward that world, and once we have done that, the divine Source Itself will arrange the rest...

It is sufficient for us to realise that we must have this attention (toward the Source), and then the rest will take care of itself. But the essential thing is this initial attention. ...Whoever wishes to reach perfection will have to pass this way. Once a person has fulfilled all the (divine) orders, the right ways will naturally open for them, and those ways will bring this attention. ...For the Truth/the Real is a single Point; there are not two.

ACTIONS, TESTS AND CONSEQUENCES: REFLECTION AND ORIENTATION

Human growth and learning, in every domain, is based on the combination of experience and reflection. In the fields of ethics and spirituality, that reflection concerns above all the observable consequences of our actions. The development of ethical and spiritual awareness, for Ostad Elahi, is no exception to this rule of trial-and-error: we learn—indeed, we may only learn—from our freely chosen risks, from our explorations of realms where we necessarily lack prior knowledge and experience, hence above all from our initial failures, confusion and mistakes. Our everyday ethical challenges and the particular personal 'tests' in which we inevitably find ourselves are gradually transformed into lasting spiritual growth precisely through our gradually expanding reflective awareness—based on both our own experiences and our careful observations of others—of the profound causal connections between the apparent 'accidents' of our destiny and the eventual inner and outer consequences of our actions.

Of course each of us encounters all sorts of philosophic and

[152] Again, *al-Ḥaqq*: *AH* 884.

religious allusions to those deeper metaphysical contexts of our ethical and spiritual life, but Ostad Elahi repeatedly points out that our most practically effective, spiritually fruitful orientation in those realms comes precisely from our own observation and active, ongoing reflection on the actual contexts and consequences of our actions. He insists that this gradual process of ethico-spiritual perfection, like all human learning, is natural, universal, and necessarily sequential:

> In consequence, if people concentrate and focus their thinking they can make great inventions in the external world, and in the spiritual world they can discover many of the secrets of being... In spiritual things the result of concentrating one's thoughts is so great that a person is able to attain their goal and to make spiritual discoveries simply by focusing their attention on that point, as long as they find the key to that enigma. The first key opens up the first problem; the second key resolves the second; and that process continues in the same way as long as that person's capability permits...[153]

Incidentally, like so many other spiritual teachers, he also constantly points out that the most visible, outward consequence of this progressive spiritual deepening is still quite 'ethical', being immediately manifest in a greater simplicity, humility and genuine attentiveness to others:

> A truly human being must make a habit of appropriate behaviour (*adab*), of love and attention to the spiritual being of the other person, no matter who it is they're dealing with, because the spiritual result of their behaviour always comes back to their own self. If the other person is also truly human, then both sides benefit from that result. But if the other party is devoid of such qualities..., then the influence of that person's misfortune and animality only affects their own self. In any case, we will always benefit from that same positive energy and spiritual benefit flowing from our own appropriate behaviour.[154]

[153] *AH* 1989.
[154] *AH* 1941.

THE UNFOLDING OF CREATIVITY AND RESPONSIBILITY

Despite the universality of the spiritual processes we have just outlined, there can be no doubt that many people (in every culture and religion) nonetheless conceive of the domain of what is 'ethical' as relatively restrained, often in terms of external norms and aims that are social, even political, in their origin and focus. Not surprisingly, Ostad Elahi—given his understanding of the natural and progressive development of our spiritual intelligence—was quite aware of the natural underpinnings of such radically differing spiritual perspectives and degrees of realisation. It is quite characteristic that his treatment of this question only serves to highlight the recurrent challenges and possibilities for further growth which this unavoidable existential situation presents:

> Just as with the other aptitudes of human beings, there are tremendous differences in human creativity, in its relative intensity or weakness. In the spiritual realm one first of all looks within oneself, concentrating and focusing one's thoughts; signs and impressions pass through one's mind. Then gradually one begins to give structure and form to those signs and impressions. And eventually that creative power can become much stronger so that a person is able to manifest those forms in spiritual discoveries and acts of grace, like those of the 'Friends of God'. If that only takes on an inner, mental form, without any external manifestation, then its effect remains limited to whatever benefit that person can derive from it within their own consciousness.[155]

This last phrase subtly highlights a further ethical—but in this context, also inevitably social and communal—implication of this process of spiritual development. For Ostad Elahi, it is evident that what flows from each person's gradually unfolding awareness of the actual spiritual context and nature of our ethical experience is not any sort of 'escape' or flight from this world, but instead an ever deeper sense of the wider challenges and responsibilities that are inseparable from that inner transformation:

[155] *AH* 1989 (includes the following quotation as well).

As a result, if we have reflected on the famous saying 'Whoever knows their self, knows their Lord'; if we've grasped how far the spiritual station of humanity actually extends; and if we've understood the full immensity of that power God has placed within us—then we can begin to see how every human being has the unique privilege and capacity to climb higher than the angels, with regard to spiritual matters, as well as to study and become educated in this external world. This human capacity is like pure fresh water hidden under the ground. If people bring that water out and make good use of it, that's wonderful; but otherwise it's wasted. So if a human being disregards that capacity, they will remain within the same limits—and they may even sink lower than an animal.

ENLIGHTENED PERSEVERANCE

One final key to the ongoing transformation of our ethical experience into spiritual realisation—implicit in everything we have discussed until now—is the indispensable element of adequate time. Like any mountain climb, the ascending spiral (the *miʿrāj*) of experience, reflection and realisation constantly broadens our perspectives. It transforms our conceptions of who we are and our awareness of the nature of the fields of space and time within which we grow and interact. The ongoing ethical response to that slowly unfolding ascension is of course the spiritual virtue of *ṣabr*, of what we only very inadequately call things like 'perseverance', 'courage', or—in the even simpler idiom of Hafez and the other great Sufi poets—'the work' (*kār*).

This inescapable dimension of the whole process of spiritual perfection is beautifully summarised, in language which intentionally evokes a deeper understanding of the central Qur'anic symbols of the eschatological 'Gardens' and the 'Fire,' in Ostad Elahi's outwardly simple story of an old farmer he once met:

> One day I was outside of town when I saw a very beautiful orchard and fields out in the middle of the desert. I asked whose it was, and they told me: 'It belongs to a person who started out with absolutely nothing and has now come to this point. One day he was passing by there when he noticed some moisture under the rocks on the surface.

He dug down a little deeper with his walking stick and saw that the wetness increased. With a great deal of toil and trouble he constructed an irrigation tunnel, and now he's been busy with that for some twenty years.'

Later I met that man, and I was very friendly and encouraging with him. As he described himself: 'When I first came here I was alone and without any money. I had just enough to buy a bucket and a shovel, but with a lot of hard work I was able to channel the water, and now I've reached this point.' All those orchards and fields he had were the result of this principle of perseverance.[156]

*

Now if this brief summary of Ostad Elahi's teaching on the ethical foundations of spiritual life has frequently recalled more familiar passages in scriptures and other spiritual teachings from any number of other religious traditions, that should not be surprising, since one of his most constantly reiterated points is that the fundamental principles of religious and spiritual reality are indeed the same and universal, constantly repeated by all the great spiritual teachers and guides in ways adapted to their own time and audiences. Yet those classical formulations of that universal Truth (of *al-Ḥaqq*, the truly Real), as we all know, can often become obscured over time by the inevitable processes of transmission, interpretation, and the use of unfamiliar symbolic language and older esoteric forms of communication. So as more of Ostad Elahi's writings gradually become accessible in other languages, it will become easier to verify to what extent he was successful in his constant aims of pointing more directly to that one Truth, without problematic symbols and allusions; of bringing out explicitly and universally what was often opaque or concealed in earlier traditions; and in re-focusing our attention on the universal 'quintessence' of the revealed religions, on the common ground of what is and remains humanly essential and true.

Hopefully these few selections have conveyed something of characteristic qualities of directness, simplicity, and explicit univer-

[156] *AH* 1936.

sality which are indeed essential characteristics of his way of teaching. As he himself put it in one of the sayings that dates from the last years of his life:

> I have not passed over any subject in silence: all that is needed is a grasp of the question and the aspiration (to understand). And that aspiration comes from the angelic soul.[157]

[157] Literally, from the (individual immortal) 'spirit' (*rūḥ*). *AH* 2073.

POSTSCRIPT

The End of Esotericism? The Changing Ecology of Spiritual Life

MANY THEMES CONNECT our three thinkers and the tasks of realisation (*taḥqīq*) each of them have suggested. One of the most central is their common stress on the universality of the challenges of our philosophic and spiritual life—a universality which consists above all in our ongoing responsibility for reflection and right action precisely in the particular, individual, constantly changing circumstances of each person's life. (Here we may recall especially al-Fārābī's concluding words at the end of Chapter One above.) Another expression for that active, applied spiritual intelligence is 'discernment': the challenge to discover, communicate and actualise intelligible spiritual principles not just in our 'inner life', but in the entire wider contexts of our lives and the ongoing consequences of our actions and intentions. There is no earthly conclusion to that task, and the appropriate response to each of these thinkers is surely to begin to make the indispensable connections between their teachings and the actual situations in which those teachings do 'become real' for each of us.

One specific consequence of these teachers' common focus on realisation is their emphasis on the necessity of carefully adapting one's forms of teaching, writing and appropriate action—of 'communication' in the broadest sense—to our actual changing circumstances, assumptions and audiences. In their own time, one of the key illustrations of that principle, for both al-Fārābī and Ibn ʿArabī, was their masterful creation of complex forms of 'esoteric' expression carefully adapted to their multiple audiences and to their particular political, cultural and religious situations: in both cases, the rhetorical forms they created remained effective and profoundly influential for centuries.[158] But a millennium separates us from

[158] See the illustrations of this point discussed in Further Reading below.

al-Fārābī, and almost eight centuries from Ibn 'Arabī, so the particular difficulties their classical forms of calculatedly indirect, highly symbolic expression pose for any modern audience are already quite evident if we simply turn from the first two chapters here to the simplicity and immediacy of Ostad Elahi's oral teachings in Chapter Three.[159] The difficulties most students and readers today, whatever their original religious and cultural background, inevitably encounter simply in understanding the intentions of such classical philosophic and spiritual writers—and from any pre-modern religion or civilisation, not just Islamic sources—are only amplified when we move on to the more fundamental challenges of actually communicating and applying those teachings beyond the boundaries of traditional religious settings, as we constantly must do in today's world.

Most of the wider changes underlying these new challenges of communication have taken place on a global scale only over the past century, indeed even more recently in much of what we still call 'the Islamic world'. So the title of this concluding section is intentionally interrogative. All I can do here is to make a few basic observations that are already quite obvious to anyone teaching and 'interpreting' in this field of religious and spiritual studies, anywhere in the world today. What comes after that observation, our three teachers would suggest, is surely not so much a matter for academic speculation, as for the construction of renewed, necessarily creative forms of effective communication.

The first observation is that many of the basic historical assumptions of the older traditions of 'esotericism'—not just as a particular form of writing, but in terms of the larger social, political and religious contexts in which those traditions operated—are simply no longer operative. Secondly, the widespread destruction of the underpinnings of traditional forms of esoteric expression is closely tied to even more far-reaching changes in the role and form of the traditional 'exoteric' religious traditions. And thirdly, the new cul-

[159] However, his own writings for learned audiences in Iran for the most part do reflect the forms and assumptions of Islamic esotericism traditionally shared by those audiences. See the illustrations of this point in our forthcoming translation of his late philosophic work '*Knowing the Spirit*' (*Maʿrifat ar-Rūḥ*), discussed in Further Reading below.

tural forms in which people everywhere are increasingly encountering and realising the perennial ends of philosophic and spiritual life are developing in parallel with the gradual emergence in a wide range of practical, intellectual and scientific contexts of what we might call a 'new science of spirituality'. Finally, it is already clear that the combined effects of these three ongoing developments have already dramatically transformed the wider operative context of spiritual teaching, anywhere in the world today. In light of those dramatic changes, which have reached many areas only within the past few decades, it is not unlikely that over a longer period of time those same developments may also transform the wider ecology of spiritual life, on a global scale, in ways we can only imagine by remote analogy with the equally novel historic emergence and transforming spread of the 'world religions' only two to three millennia earlier.

THE CHANGING CONTEXTS OF SPIRITUAL COMMUNICATION

Since our purpose here is to awaken fruitful reflection on the essential practical challenges posed by these recent historical developments, and not to describe or explain the phenomena as such (tasks which would require many volumes), a single anecdote can illustrate many of the deeper changes in question. Only a decade ago, I was first designing a study question for beginning students of the Islamic humanities, intended to help them grasp the deeper sources and intentions of those creative local forms of expression of the spiritual teachings of the Qur'an and hadith, appropriately adapted to various cultural and linguistic settings, which eventually brought about the emergence of Islam as a 'world religion'. Many of those recurrent creative expressions are familiar enough in any major religion, including spiritual music and visual arts; prayers and devotional writings; guides to spiritual practice; hagiography or lives of saints; edifying stories and sayings; lyric poetry and other forms of spiritual autobiography. Before studying classical Islamic examples of each of those broad genres of spiritual communication, the students were asked to write down a particular illustration of each of these basic forms of spiritual life already familiar to them from their own experience, and to explain something of its actual influence and effects on them. Since the individuals in question were already interested in religious studies and came each year from a wide range of Christian, Muslim, Jewish, Buddhist and other religious and cultural backgrounds, I naively expected at first that their responses would reflect cognate 'classical' forms from those other religious traditions, as inculcated by their particular childhood religious training. But that was very rarely the case. Instead their usual responses, extending over a decade, were consistently drawn almost entirely from the institutions and creations of their own ambient—often 'popular' and only rarely visibly 'religious'—culture.[160]

While part of this surprising result is no doubt connected with the wider transformations in the popular roles and understanding of religion, the more positive and useful result of this experiment was the way it highlighted four key developments involving traditionally 'esoteric' spiritual disciplines and forms of communication in recent decades: i.e., far-reaching transformations in the relative autonomy, accessibility, diversity and creativity of the traditional forms in question. The first point illustrated by those students' response was the remarkable autonomy of spiritual expressions in no way explicitly tied to any particular religious tradition, certainly not to the historically dominant local forms of Christianity. Closely tied to this was the equally astonishing diversity of relevant, individually effective forms of communication and teaching: despite understandable parental (and professorial) fears as to the 'indoctrinating' and homogenising effects of popular culture, rarely were a given student's particular answers duplicated even once in any of the many categories listed above. A third wider development well illustrated here is the extraordinary recent public accessibility of previously quite hidden modes of expression (including living artists, teachers, etc.) from various traditional religious contexts,[161] from the forms of

[160] Even individual students' infrequent references to illustrations drawn from familiar spiritual and institutional expressions of a particular religious tradition often had no discernible relationship to that particular student's own personal religious and family upbringing: Buddhist texts and teachers, or traditional Sufi musicians, for example, were frequently cited by many individuals from non-Buddhist and non-Muslim backgrounds.

[161] This point is particularly noteworthy since the social and literary forms and assumptions of esotericism, in Islam as in other religions and civilisations, had one very dramatic and obvious spiritual cost (or dubious assumption): their inherent

Tibetan Buddhism to the spiritual music, *dhikr* and rituals of many classical forms of Sufism.[162] And finally, perhaps most striking was the impressive degree of ongoing creativity of new forms and institutions of communication in each of the above-mentioned domains.

Of course the particular answers of all these individuals were coloured by their own personal circumstances and opportunities—but in ways that had far more to do with their common generational experiences of the available media and culture (increasingly global in both its sources and expressions) than with any of the once-determinative influences of their formal religious, educational and family upbringing. Sceptical observers—who might naturally and understandably suspect that the wider developments so consistently illustrated by such groups of undergraduate students were actually somehow limited in their pervasive influences to their particular country, class or educational background—would best be advised to listen seriously to their own compatriots of that same age.[163] Whatever one's local situa-

---

elitism, or apparent separation of the specialist practitioners and devoted 'experts' from the surrounding religious community. Of course that was a procedure and fundamental assumption which a number of distinguished critics and spiritual reformers—including precisely the prophetic founders of several of the religions concerned!—had themselves apparently questioned rather forcefully. Much of Ibn ʿArabī's writing, in particular, is actually devoted to a wide range of criticism of nascent 'Sufi' institutions, practices and assumptions, precisely for suggesting that the demands and responsibilities of spirituality were somehow restricted only to certain individuals or specialised small groups, rather than the entire human community.

162 The open public accessibility of the musical forms and *dhikr* rituals of Sufi and other Muslim spiritual groups, for example, is an almost unimaginably rapid recent development. Only a few years ago, I introduced my undergraduate students at Princeton, with some trepidation, to a sampling of remarkable Islamic traditions of spiritual music and *dhikr*—accumulated over years of travel and exploration, often with the help of intrepid ethnomusicologist friends—which had remained entirely secret and restricted to small circles of initiates, usually from remote mountainous and desert regions, for many centuries. Little more than a decade later, representatives of many of those until recently highly esoteric musical traditions of Islamic spiritual music, from Morocco to Indonesia, are universally available in beautifully produced CDs in the 'world music' section of any large music store, while a number of the same master-musicians are not only recording, but even giving public concerts throughout the world. (For the notable illustration of Ostad Elahi's extraordinary spiritual musicianship, see the study by J. During, and related references, in Further Reading below.)

163 To give one concrete illustration, as we have gradually experimented (always

tion, the ongoing implications of this world-wide transformation in the autonomy, diversity, accessibility and creativity of all these forms of communication constitute a demanding challenge of 'realisation' wherever we happen to live and work.

THE CHANGING ROLES OF 'RELIGION'

The traditional artistic and intellectual forms of communication that we now call 'esoteric', so consummately illustrated in the writings of both al-Fārābī and Ibn ʿArabī, obviously presupposed as their effective context a wider shared and relatively constant 'exoteric' body of accepted ritual, cultural and social forms. For more than a millennium, that wider context and shared matrix of communication has usually been provided by the local forms of one or another of the world religions.[164] One critically important aspect of that persistent religious framework of communication was the existence of a comprehensive, relatively stable cultural consensus, among the 'learned' experts in each of the traditions in question (philosophic, theological, spiritual, artistic, etc.), as to the shared canonical repertoire of symbols, vocabulary and myths which was the accepted basis for their own more creative interpretations. Now it should surprise no one to observe that there are today few places left in the world where any particular religion is still effectively available as *the sole common substrate of communication* in all the particular spiritual and cultural domains we have just mentioned.[165]

---

with considerable trepidation) with the powerfully effective use of carefully chosen films for workshops and seminars in spiritual teaching over the years—working with audiences from an ever-increasing diversity of ages and cultural, religious and social backgrounds—we have been repeatedly astonished by the extraordinary universality and efficacy of the spiritual masterpieces of that medium, cutting across all those so apparent barriers and differences.

[164] Of course in the sense of what al-Fārābī and other Muslim thinkers, following a fundamental Qur'anic distinction, very self-consciously and intentionally refer to as their local 'socio-religious grouping' (*milla*), not the one divine and universal Reality of *Dīn Allāh* and *Dīn al-Haqq*. (See the eschatological verses that close this book.)

[165] To avoid any possible misunderstanding, this is obviously not meant to say that inherited religious traditions somehow do not continue to operate as central—sometimes still as exclusive—modes of practice and perception for many individuals and small groups, in a wide number of domains. But today the price of that comforting 'exclusivity', almost anywhere, is to become proportionately closed off

The essential, very practical and unavoidable consequence of such developments for the subject of this book are very simple, if we look at that changing role of traditional religions from the perspective of an al-Fārābī, for example. In short, at the increasingly quite tangibly (not just ideally) global level of those larger human 'communities of ends' which are naturally constituted by the tasks of realising and perfecting the highest human ends, no single religion—in any of their previously existing forms, at least—can realistically provide such a comprehensive social, cultural and political framework for realisation.[166] If we briefly point out here the historically recent (and still ongoing) processes of 'disconnection' between what people still continue to call 'religions' and those actual effective communities of human realisation which are the subject and aim of our three thinkers, it is not in order to analyse, criticise or bemoan those world-historical developments in themselves. Instead, we do so here simply to highlight specifically several key areas where our new responsibilities of realisation, and the corresponding creative tasks of spiritual communication and community-building, are particularly compelling and unavoidable.

First, in much of the world we have only very recently witnessed the separation of what people now call 'religion' from the pursuit—and above all, the practice and active communication—of truth and of beauty, and thus from all the complex, rigorous artistic and scientific disciplines that those once quintessentially religious pursuits centrally involved in each world religious tradition.

The second recent development has been the even more far-reaching separation of what people now normally call 'religion' (i.e., the rituals, scriptures and basic symbols of the world religions) from the

from major areas even of local cultural life and communication, not to mention the wider world, in much the same way as monastic and other small 'intentional communities' were in the past. For one particularly rich and poignantly accessible symbolic illustration of this increasingly universal dilemma, see the extraordinary recent Tibetan Buddhist/Indian film, *The Cup*. (See also n. 167 below.)

[166] Of course this observation clearly extends to Marxism (that recent apocalyptic sectarian variant of Judeo-Christian messianic tradition), which for almost a century claimed to provide just such an ecumenical global framework for a potentially transformed human community. Students of Islamic philosophy are well aware of the little-known historical threads linking al-Fārābī, in particular, to such recent developments.

forms of 'natural contemplation' and those common socio-economic structures which were inseparable from the regular patterns and inescapable conditions of world-wide agrarian life. That is to say, many of the most central symbols and rituals of the world religions were once deeply rooted in most human beings' direct life-experience of their surrounding world of nature and in shared conditions of economic and social life visibly rooted in those given natural conditions.

This rapidly disappearing matrix of shared life-conditions underlying traditional forms of religious ritual and symbolism included such fundamental realities as: (i) constant reminders of our immediate dependency on nature (through the decisive vicissitudes of weather, famine, plagues, fertility and infant mortality). (ii) The self-evident regularity of those natural processes and the corresponding contexts of 'natural symbolism' immediately mirroring in those visible processes the deeper laws and invisible realities of the spiritual world. (iii) Constant reminders of our mutually dependent connections (both life-sustaining and symbolic) with a much wider community of other natural creatures. (iv) The universal analogies between the visible socio-cultural hierarchies of the agrarian socio-economic pyramid and the active orders of the spiritual realm. And (v) the direct experience of our innate spiritual powers of communication, prayer and inspiration (i.e., of the natural awakening of the spiritual senses) which arises spontaneously out of that solitude and deep silence which were once almost universal, yet are now often beyond price in much of the contemporary world.

A third recent global development is the mysterious widespread popularisation of the notion that religions in general are somehow narrowly restricted 'belief systems', curiously restricted first to an increasingly narrow set of specifiable symbols and rituals, which are then additionally assumed to be timeless and historically unchanging. The obvious result of such widespread popular notions, given the unprecedented transformations of the present-day world, is that 'religions'—once they have become so narrowly and inadequately conceived—quickly appear as almost unbridgeably distant from the vast majority of spiritually operative symbols and rituals in any actual ambient culture, wherever one may live.[167]

[167] Throughout the 'Islamic world', in particular, the profound penetration of

A final, inescapable development—and at the same time a powerful historical vehicle for carrying out the above-mentioned transformations—has been the widespread, still ongoing reduction of the traditional world religions to particular narrow political ideologies (or so-called 'orthodoxies'), whose empty slogans and sectarian fantasies serve as inviting rhetorical refuges for those understandably disoriented and traumatised by unprecedented social, economic and cultural changes. For millennia, of course, the localised equivalents of such politico-ideological programs and 'refuge-communities' have existed as small parts of a much wider available spectrum of alternative ways of living and perceiving within each of the world religions. But under current social, nation-state conditions—and given the increasingly radical limits, just mentioned, on what now publicly counts as 'religious'—those ideologies often have the ultimate ironic result of placing even historically long-standing and relatively universalistic traditional forms of religious life and expression in an endangered minority position (vis-à-vis the dominant ideological forms) like that once occupied by the most extreme sects and cults.

The practical consequences and choices poised by these global developments are quite diverse, and certainly not mutually exclusive. And much always depends, practically speaking, on the available means and opportunities in each particular situation. At one extreme, some are challenged to work to 'restore' and reintegrate the multiple human dimensions of once-integral religious traditions lost or destroyed as a result of the changes just enumerated.[168] But choos-

---

such previously unimaginable ideological notions over the past century is strikingly evident in the almost universal replacement in religious discourse, from the most learned to the most popular, of the central Qur'anic expression *al-dīn* (the common relation of *all* human beings to their One Source) by various forms of the word '*islam*'—used of course as a narrowly historicist cultural reference, completely divorced from its original universal Qur'anic contexts and historically accepted meanings. Such radical transformations are of course universal, and equally apparent in the profusion of increasingly sectarian, highly limited uses of the adjective '*christian*' in many contemporary Western settings.

[168] A dramatic illustration of this response that we can all now frequently witness, at the individual level, is the partial *reversal* of the old 'normal' relations between the esoteric and the exoteric aspects of religious life: that is, increasing numbers of individuals in all parts of the world self-consciously choosing to practice and live out some of the traditional forms of a particular religious

ing to work, create and teach *only* within such a limited context, in the many situations where the effective role of religious traditions has become so severely restricted, entails severe restrictions on the actual lives and range of influences one can actually affect. At the other extreme, working to realise actual awareness of those higher human ends which have been abandoned by the recently truncated 'official', ideological forms of religion, in many cases, obliges us to seek out more effective, creative possibilities rooted in the actually operative symbols and institutions of the wider world civilisation that is gradually coming into being precisely as a result of such scattered creative efforts. To take one telling example, we have only to compare the potential level of lasting impact—quantitative as well as qualitative—of almost any new book, in any language, with that of a spiritually effective and unforgettable film accessible in every culture, in order to have some sense of the spectrum of new possibilities that are emerging in these transformed historical circumstances.

THE 'NEW SCIENCE' OF SPIRITUALITY[169]

A third dimension of these wider historical transformations mentioned above, appearing on a more academic level, is what has been called the emerging 'New Science' of spirituality. Like the similarly nascent fields of global ecology and environmental studies, it appears at present as the practical converging point of a number of

tradition—not because they have simply inherited it or been born into it, but because they have gradually come to recognize the concrete, practical spiritual efficacy of its practices, symbols and rituals. This familiar contemporary phenomenon has nothing to do with older popular or learned notions of 'conversion', as the individuals in such situations typically remain quite consciously part of their wider original 'ethno-religious' communities and surroundings, carefully differentiating practically as well as intellectually between these two very different dimensions of 'religion'—or between inherited socio-cultural 'religious identity' and their particular active 'spiritual tradition'.

[169] The later Islamic philosophic discipline of 'theoretical spirituality' (*ʿirfān-i naẓarī*), whose highest achievement was the massive, but practically incomplete, philosophic edifice of Ṣadr al-dīn al-Shīrāzī ('Mullā Ṣadrā'), was a remarkable step in this direction in its own time; but unfortunately it became reduced primarily to the subject of endless purely scholastic elaboration in subsequent centuries. See the long Introduction to our *The Wisdom of the Throne: An Introduction to the Philosophy of Mulla Sadra* (Princeton, 1981), especially the discussion of Sadra's 'logic of transcendence' and the wider spiritual and political intentions informing all his writing.

hitherto disparate sciences and related 'arts' and areas of spiritual and therapeutic practice. On a world-wide scale, its initial developments at this time are comparable in many respects to the condition of the nascent social sciences, chemistry or biological sciences only a few centuries ago—all of which likewise began with the careful (if to us now seemingly primitive) attempts at gathering and systematically classifying the relevant natural phenomena, while very hesitantly seeking appropriate hypothetical models and explanations.[170] This similarity is strikingly evident if we compare the contemporary writings available in the relevant fields with the (to our modern eyes) often quaint and partial phenomenologies of economic and social laws and realities to be found in Ibn Khaldun's famous *Muqaddima* (and the rest of his *History*), in Montesquieu's *l'Esprit des Lois*, or in Vico's *New Science.*

The first, most visible aspect of this new development is that the religious and historical sciences (and their contemporary offshoots among the social sciences) are making possible an ever wider and more encompassing empirical phenomenology of spiritual practice and experience, and of the corresponding traditional theoretical explanations.

Even beginners in this field now have easily accessible an extraordinary, rapidly growing repertoire—and eventually, for those seriously interested, a potential deeper synthesis—of millennia of ongoing 'spiritual research' extending to an increasingly global range of cultures, practices and creeds.[171] The longer-term public interest and wider impact of that historical research, of course, lies in its fruitful intersection with related contemporary forms of practice

[170] The serial transformations of the field of 'geology' over the past 150 years—most dramatically, within the past half-century—offer another fascinating parallel example of this wider, ongoing process of scientific development: see John McPhee's popular, but no less revealing, presentation in *Annals of the Former World* (New York, Farrar, Strauss and Giroux, 1998).

[171] The new explicitly moral and spiritual motivation, and the self-consciously global focus of those pursuing this discipline on its immediate *practical* relevance to all these essential human tasks, make this emerging science something fundamentally different from the 19th-century historicist project of a study of 'comparative religions'—even though the much wider contemporary discipline clearly builds on and integrates the achievements and discoveries of those earlier historical and anthropological researchers.

and scientific research which are only in their earliest stages.

Thus, in the related domains of psychology—in the very broadest sense of that term—we are faced with such new fields of research and practice as the increasingly extensive study of 'near-death experiences' (and eventually of the much broader spectrum of 'para-normal' spiritual phenomena); the cross-culturally convergent discoveries emerging from hypnotic regression therapy (and a host of parallel phenomena arising in the practice of many other widespread 'body-centred' therapies); cross-civilisational studies of the spiritual and imaginal lives of children, of organically inexplicable forms of 'mental illness', out-of-body experiences and other altered states of consciousness, and so on. What is striking in each of these cases is two mutually reinforcing processes of convergence: the way in which initially isolated and *ad hoc*, empirically based forms of practice, therapy and bodies of experience almost immediately demand a wider intellectual and spiritual framework of understanding; and at the same time, the way narrowly focused scientific and objective approaches to any of the particular phenomena in these fields quickly come to encounter the unfamiliar and much more problematic, deeply complex reality of their wholistic spiritual contexts. Finally, even in the more sceptical domains of official medicine and the biological sciences, under the competing pressure of growing popular interest in many forms of 'alternative medicine' drawn from various civilisations and earlier spiritual traditions, we are witnessing the first fascinating 'empirical' studies—that is, in terms of the accepted methodologies of modern science—of the actual long-term effects of prayer, music, meditation, fasting and a host of other age-old spiritual disciplines and practices universally associated with more traditional forms of healing, therapy and spiritual realisation.

THE CRUCIBLE OF CONSCIENCE

What happens—what as yet unsuspected possibilities are brought into being—when all of these different parallel developments we have briefly mentioned here are brought together at the same time, as they actually are for most young people growing up anywhere in the world today? One way of at least conceiving of those possibilities is to start with a closely analogous area which is in fact really part of the larger process we are trying to understand: that is, with the very similar transformations and gamut of responses which are perhaps more clearly visible (and surely less controversial) in the related area of our global physical, natural and environmental interdependence.

There, to begin with, recent decades have witnessed phenomenal growth in the number of students pursuing the new major fields of 'environmental studies' or 'ecological studies'. The development of those new disciplines of broad-based ecological study and praxis is practically driven by the urgent integration of what were previously viewed as quite separate disciplines (across the natural, biological and social and political sciences), as individuals with vision struggle to acquire an adequately informed awareness of the conditions of the increasingly evident ecological interdependence of our actual global community. For that sort of new science and integrated vision is clearly indispensable if we are to make truly responsible and lastingly effective political and economic decisions at that global level—and certainly at more local levels as well. In this quite publicly visible domain, we can clearly see how everyone is haltingly beginning to recognise—almost by force, as it were, and in unavoidably concrete ways—very real world-wide moral and spiritual unities which were once visible only to the great philosophers, saints and visionary 'dreamers'.

Now all the recent religious and spiritual phenomena we have just enumerated above can easily be seen as both the symptoms and the ongoing causes of very similar responses in the explicitly moral and spiritual domain. Today what happens in and to Sarajevo (or Kosovo, or Jerusalem, or…)—so visibly, inescapably witnessed around the world—can no longer be treated simply as the 'foreign affairs' of 'strangers', since the matrix of human communities to which we already belong and in which we actually participate already extends far beyond any official political mechanisms (or formally religious institution) that have yet come into existence. So it is equally apparent that the increasing numbers of students and scholars pursuing the new sciences of 'religious studies' are being pushed and pulled by very similar motives to integrate all the humanities and social and historical sciences, and the related branches of psychology, biology, medicine and other therapies, within a similarly practical global perspective, in ways that only the very new discipline of religious studies is still normally allowed to do within academia today. For those students and seekers drawn to these interrelated studies already intuitively know what they will need to learn and understand, so that they can actually begin to discover—and then act upon and communicate—those universal moral and spiritual principles which we all know 'must be there', somehow and in ways that have yet to be visibly created, in order for this emerging world civilisation to become as well a genuine moral and spiritual community.

What each of these parallel (or quite possibly converging) academic and intellectual developments have in common is the very real and exceedingly practical world-wide context from which they emerge: what one might call, adapting a central Qur'anic symbol, the increasingly global 'crucible of conscience'. That is to say, people have always been intimately familiar, at the most basic levels of families, villages, quarters and tribes; and educated elites have long been aware, in a more episodic and partial way, at the more abstract level of cultures, states and civilisations—of the painful, inevitably heated ways we actually discover our common, truly human moral and spiritual values. And then, with difficulty and constant reworking, with the ways we gradually refine and forge those hard-won discoveries into enduring moral and spiritual communities. What is different today is above all the way the most ordinary people, often with nothing *but* spiritual resources, are inevitably thrown into that intense crucible on a much wider and unavoidable scale. So today it is no exaggeration to say that virtually anyone in this world—at the level of their *conscience*, whatever their practical means of information and realistic field of action—has to come to terms somehow with the initially confusing, yet inescapable multiplicity of historically inherited religions, cultures and civilisations. And that we are all inevitably challenged to forge out of that apparent chaos a new moral and spiritual order, at least in our 'city within', in ways that were only intermittently demanded, in the past, of a relative handful of philosophers, metaphysicians and spiritual visionaries.

Some of the most potentially helpful of those philosophers and visionaries, of course, have just been introduced. And they continue to remind us that the 'end' of this wider spiritual process, the true 'Day of Rising', has always been visible from a sufficiently far-sighted perspective, for those with the requisite insight, intention, and 'eyes that can see'. Near the close of his fascinating treatise *Revealing the Results of the Spiritual Journeys*,[172] Ibn 'Arabi lets slip just such a prophetic observation about the people of faith who are living here closer to that 'end of (earthly) time'. Their native virtue and spiritual motivation, he explains, will by then have become so weakened that—like the injured and exhausted players at the end of a very long game—they need a little extra help from the 'sidelines' if they are to successfully finish their period at all:

> The time today isn't like times in the past, because it's closer to the realm of the next world, so that its people experience *more* spiritual unveiling... So the people of this time, today, are quicker to experience unveiling, more likely to witness spiritual things, more spiritually aware, and more complete in their realisation—but also more deficient in their (right) actions than in earlier times, because they are farther in time from the Companions in their witnessing the Prophet... For (right) actions were more predominant in the past, while spiritual knowing is more predominant in this time of ours, and that (expansion of spiritual awareness) will continue on increasing until the descent of Jesus—Peace be upon him (at the end of time)!

*

[172] *Kitāb al-Isfār ʿan Natā'ij al-Asfār*, in *Rasā'il Ibn ʿArabī* (Hyderabad, 1948), Part II, pages 7-8 (separately numbered). We should emphasise that Ibn 'Arabi's full discussion here at this point in no way suggests any sort of optimistic 'progress' or effortless universal spiritual advancement (as in *The Celestine Prophecies* and the like) throughout this declining course of time. Indeed he makes it very clear that he is only speaking of the increasingly *smaller* number of the *ṣāliḥūn*, those rare souls who are genuinely virtuous or spiritually apt, in that later age when he says *'a single rukʿa of prayer will be the equivalent of a lifetime of devotion earlier* (i.e., nearer the time of the Prophet)', because of the massive extent of spiritual corruption (*fasād*). As he explains there, only a relatively few souls will remain on earth at that time who are still prepared to bear the true knowing of God, so that their individual share of spiritual witnessing and unveiling will be proportionately much greater.

For Ibn 'Arabī, the same observation—and our appropriate response—were already clearly foreshadowed in the following eschatological Sura, which is traditionally considered one of the very last revelations:

بِسْمِ ٱللَّهِ ٱلرَّحْمَٰنِ ٱلرَّحِيمِ * إِذَا جَآءَ نَصْرُ ٱللَّهِ وَٱلْفَتْحُ * وَرَأَيْتَ ٱلنَّاسَ

يَدْخُلُونَ فِى دِينِ ٱللَّهِ أَفْوَاجًا * فَسَبِّحْ بِحَمْدِ رَبِّكَ وَٱسْتَغْفِرْهُ إِنَّهُۥ كَانَ تَوَّابًا *

When God's decisive support and the Opening have come,
and you[173] *see the people entering into God's Religion in waves:*
then sing forth the praise of your Sustainer and seek His forgiveness;
for surely He returns (to us) again and again.

(Sura *an-Naṣr*, 110:1-3)

[173] English does not begin to capture the intensity here—given the Source of these imperatives—of the intimate singular, unavoidably personal 'you' in question, and its threefold repetition (the last two expressed within the Arabic imperative): see the parallel explanations in our Preface on the dedicatory line from Hafez.

Further Reading

THE POTENTIAL WIDER influence of many of the classics of Islamic thought has been severely hampered by the virtual non-existence, in so many fields, of useful translations prepared in view of the needs and background of any wider, non-specialist audience. For almost all of the great thinkers concerned, given the unfamiliarity of their distinctive forms of writing and assumptions for all but a handful of academic specialists in the modern world, any useful translation in fact has to include at a minimum adequate introductory background material and detailed footnote explanations of the actual and multiple intended meanings of key words and passages, amounting to an extensive commentary. That is a daunting task, and those demanding explanatory frameworks, incidentally, have become just as indispensable for most Arabic or Persian readers today. For each of our three teachers, we have begun here with recent translations, then the most useful contextual and analytical studies for non-specialists, and finally the useful works or sources concerning the ongoing historical influences of each author. More complete scholarly bibliographies, including works in all relevant languages, can be found in many of the recent volumes cited below. Given the introductory nature of this volume, the following list is largely restricted to English-language materials, although a number of the key studies included (especially for Ibn ʿArabī) originally appeared in French.

AL-FĀRĀBĪ AND HIS PHILOSOPHIC INTERPRETERS

The broadest—and likewise the most complex—account of philosophy and political philosophy by al-Fārābī is that which he gives in his trilogy on *Attaining Happiness*, translated by M. Mahdi as *Alfarabi's Philosophy of Plato and Aristotle* (Ithaca, Cornell University Press, revised ed. 2001). Partial translations (by M. Mahdi and F. Najjar) of the opening part of that trilogy and several other important writings are conveniently included in *Medieval Political Philosophy: A Sourcebook*, ed. M. Mahdi and R. Lerner (Ithaca,

Cornell University Press, 1972); however, the restrictions of the sourcebook format mean that the introductions and annotation are very limited.

Reliable translations by Charles Butterworth of several key 'exoteric' political works of al-Fārābī are now available in the volume *The Political Writings: Selected Aphorisms and Other Texts* (Ithaca, Cornell University Press, 2001). This includes, in addition to al-Fārābī's *Fuṣūl*, his *Book of Religion*, his complete *Enumeration of the Sciences* and his *Harmonisation of the Views of Aristotle and Plato.* The same Press also plans to publish in 2003 another large volume of key translations by Butterworth devoted to several of al-Fārābī's more challenging programmatic works, including a new and complete translation of *The Political Regime*, the remarkable *K. al-Ḥurūf* ('*Book of Letters*') and his *Summary of Plato's Laws.* A final translation volume, planned for 2004, will include M. Mahdi's long-awaited translation of *The Principles of the Inhabitants of the Virtuous City*; earlier translated versions present numerous problems.

The best introduction to al-Fārābī's philosophy for the first-time reader of his work is now M. Mahdi's comprehensive study, *Alfarabi and the Foundation of Islamic Political Philosophy* (Chicago, University of Chicago Press, 2001); a shorter summary of Mahdi's interpretations can be found in his article 'Alfarabi', pp. 182-202 in *History of Political Philosophy*, ed. L. Strauss and J. Cropsey (Chicago, Rand McNally, 1972). For more advanced readers, a helpful overview of the many contrasting interpretations of al-Fārābī's thought, and of the place of his strikingly different kinds of writings (commentaries on Aristotle, political works, etc.) within those possible interpretive frameworks, is provided by M. Galston's *Politics and Excellence: The Political Philosophy of Alfarabi* (Princeton, Princeton University Press, 1990). One recent appropriately detailed illustration of how al-Fārābī's works can be read is J. Parens' *Metaphysics as Rhetoric: Alfarabi's Summary of Plato's "Laws"* (Albany, SUNY Press, 1995). Readers primarily interested in al-Fārābī as a serious philosopher should familiarise themselves with all the above writings before delving into the extensive scholarly literature which approaches al-Fārābī from a more strictly philological perspective, focusing especially on his many commentaries on works of Aristotle and on the details of his historical role in the translation and assimilation of Hellenistic thought in the early Islamic context.

The centrality of al-Fārābī's philosophic and political perspectives throughout later Islamic thought (and not simply in the self-consciously 'philosophic' traditions) down to the present day is not even remotely suggested by any of the introductory 'histories' and short surveys of Islamic philosophy, which also tend to be uneven in many other respects. For example, the fundamental role of al-Fārābī's teachings in actually inspiring and guiding what have subsequently most often been taken as some of the more original, 'anti-Aristotelian' (or 'Neoplatonic') and more openly 'religious' innovations in the influential writings of Avicenna (Ibn Sīnā) is carefully detailed in our study of 'The Philosopher-Prophet in Avicenna's Political Philosophy', pp. 152-198 in *The Political Aspects of Islamic Philosophy*, ed. C. Butterworth (Cambridge, Harvard University Press, 1992). (The wider ongoing influences of al-Fārābī's thought are also highlighted in several other studies in the same volume.) In particular, the transmission of al-Fārābī's political ideas—especially his central philosophic treatment of prophecy and religion from Avicenna through Ṭūsī to Ibn Khaldūn is detailed in our forthcoming study 'An Arab "Machiavelli"?: Rhetoric, Philosophy and Politics in Ibn Khaldun's Critique of Sufism. to appear in the proceedings of the Harvard Ibn Khaldun Conference (ed. Roy Mottahedeh, Cambridge, 2004).

In contrast, the important role of al-Fārābī's teachings is usually more carefully discussed in the vast scholarly literature on the two later Andalusian philosophers Averrroes (Ibn Rushd) and Maimonides, because of their wide and lasting influences in subsequent Western thought. Accessible translations of key writings which helpfully highlight al-Fārābī's inspiration for both philosophers can be found in *Ethical Writings of Maimonides*, tr. C. Butterworth and R. Weiss (New York, Dover, 1983) and in C. Butterworth's recent translation of Averroes' *Decisive Treatise and Epistle Dedicatory: Determining the Connection Between the Law and Wisdom* (BYU Press, 2001), along with the same scholar's translations and studies of Averroes' treatises on rhetoric that emphasise the broader Farabian framework of his political thought. A general, but still invaluable historical contextualisation of al-Fārābī's influence is provided in S. Pines' magisterial Introduction to his translation of Maimonides' *The Guide of the Perplexed* (Chicago, University of Chicago Press, 1974), supplemented more recently by R. Lerner's *Maimonides' Empire of Light: Popular Enlightenment in an Age of Belief* (Chicago, University of Chicago Press, 2000). (All the above works give further bibliographic references to the extensive relevant scholarly literature and additional translations.) Finally, the ongoing influence of al-Fārābī's thought in the Islamic West is masterfully illustrated in M. Mahdi's classic *Ibn Khaldūn's Philosophy of History: A Study in the Philosophic Foundation of the Science of Culture* (Chicago, University of Chicago Press, rev. ed. 1971).

Western scholarship has until recently largely ignored al-Fārābī's ongoing influences in those traditions of Islamic philosophy—almost all rooted in the writings of Avicenna—which have flourished down to the present throughout the Eastern (non-Arab) Islamic world. After Avicenna, the most influential historical figure in their transmission was above all the philosopher-astronomer and masterful politician Naṣīr al-Dīn al-Ṭūsī, whose political philosophy is articulated above all—usually in an ongoing dialogue and polemic with the dogmatic theologian Fakhr al-Rāzī—in his extensive, life-long commentary on Avicenna's *K. al-Ishārāt* (the political part corresponding above all to the final, supposedly 'Sufi' sections of the *Ishārāt*). Ṭūsī's influential ethical work (especially *The Nasirean Ethics*, tr. G.M. Wickens. London, Allen & Unwin, 1964) explicitly refers to his programmatic debts to al-Fārābī, particularly al-Fārābī's famous *Fuṣūl.* See also J. Walbridge, 'The Political Thought of Quṭb al-Dīn al-Shīrāzī' (al-Ṭūsī's most important disciple), in *The Political Aspects of Islamic Philosophy*, pp. 345-378.

More recently, al-Fārābī's political perspectives were particularly influential in the writings and other work of two lastingly influential later Islamic philosophers, Ṣadr al-Dīn al-Shīrāzī ('Mullā Ṣadrā') in Iran, and Shāh Walī Allāh of Delhi, in the Indian subcontinent.[174] Our emphasis on the framework of political philosophy informing Mulla Sadra's thought, elaborated throughout the general

[174] The political and philosophic influences of al-Fārābī are even more visible in the influential work and teaching of the contemporary Pakistani philosopher and

Introduction to *The Wisdom of the Throne: An Introduction to the Philosophy of Mulla Sadra* (Princeton, Princeton University Press, 1980)—a perspective which was then considered quite unorthodox—was dramatically confirmed by the highly visible subsequent efforts of the well-known professor and lifelong student of Sadra's works who went on to lead the most recent Iranian revolution and to found institutions often openly inspired by classical Islamic philosophic models.

IBN ᶜARABĪ AND HIS INTERPRETERS

The relative profusion of translations, biographies and studies of Ibn ᶜArabī and his writings in recent years has created something of a fortunate dilemma for those readers, new to his work, who might want to explore its many facets and the perspectives suggested here. A good starting point for his actual writings is the extensive anthology of translations by J. Morris and W. Chittick, *Ibn 'Arabī: The Meccan Revelations* (NY, Pir Press, 2002), including a new Introduction intended for first-time readers. In addition to the other studies and translations already mentioned in earlier notes, the following suggestions, for those without any prior background in Ibn ᶜArabī or the many related Islamic spiritual and philosophic traditions, are limited to English language books, although readers at home in Spanish will now find a number of important recent translations (including works not yet available in English or French) by Pablo Beneito, Victor Palleja and others, a happy sign of increasing interest in this native son who—like his near-contemporary Moses de Leon—must surely be counted among the most enduring contributors to world civilisation and religious understanding.

For Ibn ᶜArabī's life, immediate historical context and a basic summary of his central teachings, one can now readily recommend S. Hirtenstein's *The Unlimited Mercifier: The spiritual life and thought of Ibn ᶜArabī* (Oxford, Anqa and White Cloud Press, 1999), which is the first volume explicitly designed to introduce these

---

reformer, Fazlur Rahman, while M. Mahdi over the years has also highlighted the pervasive influences of al-Fārābī's ideas on a number of other historically influential Islamic activists and reformers, notably J. al-Dīn 'al-Afghānī' and his famous colleagues.

points to a general, non-academic English-speaking audience; the numerous photographs of the cities and sites where Ibn ᶜArabī lived, taught and prayed are especially helpful for anyone unfamiliar with those cultural centres of the Islamic world. C. Addas' *Quest for the Red Sulphur: The Life of Ibn 'Arabī* (Cambridge, The Islamic Texts Society, 1993), ably translated into English, is a longer, slightly more academic introduction to the same subjects, giving greater detail on Ibn ᶜArabī's own teachers and cultural roots in different fields of medieval Islamic scholarship and Sufism. For Ibn ᶜArabī's own vivid depiction of his earliest Spanish and North African teachers, companions and friends on the Sufi path, R. Austin's *Sufis of Andalusia* (London, Allen & Unwin, 1971) remains an indispensable and endlessly fascinating source.[175] Finally, W. Chittick's *The Sufi Path of Knowledge: Ibn al-'Arabi's Metaphysics of the Imagination* (Albany, SUNY, 1989), offers a voluminously illustrated, detailed and clearly structured introduction—based on hundreds of shorter translations from the *Futūḥāt*—to virtually all the key facets of Ibn ᶜArabī's teaching.

For the 'Bezels of Wisdom' (*Fuṣūṣ al-Ḥikam*) and the subsequent Islamic traditions of commentary, probably the most readable (and certainly the most comprehensible and clearly explained) introduction remains T. Izutsu's pioneering *A Comparative Study of the Key Philosophical Concepts in Sufism and Taoism: Ibn 'Arabī and Lao-Tzū, Chuang-Tzū* (Tokyo, Keio Institute, 1966),[176] despite its reliance on the more Avicennan philosophic commentary tradition of al-Kāshānī. For the novice in this field, the English translation of T. Burckhardt's original French version of a few key selected chapters of the *Fuṣūṣ*, *The Wisdom of the Prophets* (Oxford, Beshara, 1975) is considerably more approachable than R. Austin's *Ibn al-Arabi:*

[175] Readers of the Austin translation should also try to consult the missing translation of the Introductory section of the same work ('Excerpts from the Epistle on the Spirit of Holiness (*Risālah Rūḥ al-Quds*)', tr. R. Boase and F. Sahnoun) in *Muhyiddin Ibn 'Arabi: A Commemorative Volume*, ed. S. Hirtenstein and M. Tiernan (Shaftesbury, Element, 1993). That volume also contains seventeen other important translations and critical studies. Austin's book is still available, through the Ibn 'Arabi Society, in the reprinted edition by Beshara Publishers, 1988.

[176] Still available in the later version published by the University of California Press, 1984, under the new title: *Sufism and Taoism: A Comparative Study of Key Philosophic Concepts.*

The Bezels of Wisdom (New York, Paulist Press, 1980)—which has long helpful prefaces to each chapter. Ron Nettler's *Sufi Metaphysics and the Qur'anic Prophets: Ibn 'Arabī's Thought and Method in the 'Fuṣūṣ al-Ḥikam'*, a helpful volume of commentary on the *Fuṣūṣ*, including newly translated material, is now available from The Islamic Texts Society (Cambridge, 2003).

An ever-increasing number of studies (see below) have elaborated the far-reaching influences of this work and its commentators throughout later Islamic culture and religious life, from the Balkans to China and Indonesia. See, among others, the voluminous anthology of related texts from many key figures in the later Islamic humanities (though the subtitle might suggest something quite different) included in S. Murata's *The Tao of Islam: A Sourcebook on Gender Relationships in Islamic Thought* (Albany, SUNY, 1992); the four-volume English version of later Turkish commentaries on the *Fuṣūṣ*, translated as *Ismail Hakki Bursevi's translation of and commentary on Fuṣūṣ al-Ḥikam*, (Oxford, MIAS, 1986); and perhaps most fascinating, S. Murata's recent far-reaching study of several earlier Neo-Confucian Chinese Muslim thinkers profoundly influenced by Ibn 'Arabī, *Chinese Gleams of Sufi Light* (Albany, SUNY, 2000).

On a more widely accessible level, M. Sells' *Stations of Desire: Love Elegies From Ibn 'Arabi* (Jerusalem, Ibis, 2000) should now replace R. Nicholson's frequently cited versions (*The Tarjuman al-Ashwaq: A Collection of Mystical Odes*) as a superb introduction to the central poetic dimension of Ibn ᶜArabī's work, which is of course quite evident in the 'keynote' poems that introduce every chapter of the *Meccan Illuminations.* The even more recent translations of Ibn ᶜArabī's prayers by S. Hirtenstein and P. Beneito, *The Seven Days of the Heart* (Oxford, Anqa, 2001) suggest something of the profound spiritual and devotional practice underlying and always assumed in Ibn ᶜArabī's writings; the translators' introduction is especially helpful in that regard. And our thematic studies and translations included in the forthcoming *The Reflective Heart: Discovering Spiritual Intelligence in Ibn 'Arabī's 'Meccan Illuminations'* (forthcoming, 2004), together with another planned volume of translations of Ibn ᶜArabī's powerful shorter writings on practical spirituality, *Spiritual Practice and Discernment*, should help to make this central dimension of Ibn ʿArabī's work more widely accessible.

A more demanding, but absolutely fundamental and ground-breaking work on Ibn ʿArabī's understanding of 'Sainthood' (*walāya*)—a study that has become indispensable for understanding the spiritual and conceptual underpinnings of this central feature of popular Islamic devotion and piety in every corner of the Islamic world, even today—is M. Chodkiewicz's *The Seal of the Saints: Prophethood and Sainthood in the doctrine of Ibn 'Arabī* (Cambridge, The Islamic Texts Society, 1993), ably translated but still to be studied in the original if at all possible. Finally, G. Elmore's recent study and translation of Ibn ʿArabī's early *ʿAnqā' Mughrib*, *Islamic Sainthood in the Fulness of Time: Ibn al-'Arabī's 'Book of the Fabulous Gryphon'* (Leiden, Brill, 2000) well illustrates the many challenges of deciphering, much less 'translating', the extraordinarily cryptic earlier poetic and symbolic writings from Andalusia and N. Africa which preceded the composition of the '*Meccan Illuminations*'.

The most extensive translations of the *Futūḥāt* to appear recently are W. Chittick's two massive volumes, *The Sufi Path of Knowledge* (details above) and *The Self-Disclosure of God: Principles of Ibn al-ʿArabī's Cosmology* (Albany, SUNY, 1998), to be followed eventually by an equally long volume of translations on related areas of his cosmogony and ontology. Complementary to those translations—in that they focus on the humanly 'immediate', active dimensions of eschatology, spiritual realisation and Ibn ʿArabī's phenomenology of spiritual life—are a planned series of volumes on the *Futūḥāt*, including translations and studies originally delivered as public lectures and conference papers over the past decade, which we hope to publish in book form in the near future. These include the translations of the eschatological chapters 59-65 and 271 (plus related passages from other chapters), already promised in our original translations from the *Futūḥāt* (*Ibn ʿArabī's 'Divine Comedy': Eschatology and Realisation in the Meccan Illuminations*) and *The Traveller and the Way: 'Wandering" and the Spiritual Journey'* (a translation and commentary of his *Risālat al-Isfār*, plus several chapters on the same theme from the *Futūḥāt*). Indeed the level of scholarly understanding and world-wide interest in the *Futūḥāt* has approached the point where the possibility of a serious, collective effort to begin to translate in its entirety at least the opening 'Section' (*faṣl al-maᶜārif*: roughly a quarter of the entire work) is now being seriously considered. Such a task should be realisable within the next few decades.

Anyone wishing to keep up with translations and studies of Ibn ᶜArabī, and more particularly with the dramatic unfolding of world-wide academic research into his profound influences in all aspects of later Islamic religion and the Islamic humanities, should refer to past and present issues of the *Journal of the Muhyiddin Ibn 'Arabī Society*, Oxford (now into its third decade). With contributions that have often been delivered first by renowned scholarly specialists, increasingly from all regions of the Islamic world, at the two international Symposia sponsored by the Ibn 'Arabi Society each year (at Oxford and Berkeley), the *Journal* has helped to create an active global network of scholars, students and translators whose impact is increasingly evident in, among other fields, the number of international conferences now devoted to the 'Greatest Master' and his later Muslim interpreters each year. This world-wide collective effort to rediscover the profound influences of Ibn ᶜArabī and his teachings on central dimensions of Islamic culture from W. Africa to China and Indonesia is not just an academic project of historical 'archaeology': those involved, in each country and region concerned, are well aware of the contemporary and future significance of Ibn ᶜArabī's understanding of the roots of Islamic spirituality and tradition for any lasting effort of renewal and revivification within Islam and the emerging global civilisation.

Finally, the truly great books in this field, as in any other, do not age, but only stand out more vividly with the passage of time. The following two classic volumes—both originally published in French, although fortunately available in solid English translations[177]—were certainly not intended for 'beginners' in the sense we began with above. Both are the mature, richly evocative and moving fruits of an

[177] Because both works are so highly allusive, personal, poetic, and so deeply rooted in very personal readings of difficult passages from Ibn ᶜArabī, the Qur'an and many other Islamic classics, they should certainly be read in the original if at all possible.

intensely personal, life-long reflection on the central issues and perspectives of all of Ibn ʿArabī's accessible writings, with visions and emphases that are radically different, yet ultimately astonishingly complementary. The first is Henry Corbin's *Creative Imagination in the Sufism of Ibn ʿArabī*; the second is Michel Chodkiewicz's *An Ocean Without Shore: Ibn ʿArabī, the Book and the Law* (Albany, SUNY, 1993).[178] One could readily apply to both those remarkable works what Ibn ʿArabī says of his own *Meccan Illuminations* and his ideal readers in those key passages of his *Introduction* cited above (n. 54): the essential preparedness such works require is not simply, or even primarily, academic. Reading them gives a real sense of how diverse, yet powerfully transforming, the influences of Ibn ʿArabī have been and will continue to be.

OSTAD ELAHI

The most detailed—and highly insightful—biographical study of the remarkable life of Ostad Elahi and the original context of his teaching, focusing primarily on his extraordinary accomplishments as a musician,[179] is certainly Jean During's recent *L'âme des sons: L'art unique d'Ostad Elahi (1895-1974)*, Gordes, le Relié, 2001; an English translation is in preparation. During's magisterial study is helpfully complemented by the large volume of photos, personal accounts and other biographical background entitled *Unicity: Ostad Elahi, 1895-1974*, which was published on the occasion of the international UNESCO commemoration of his centenary (Paris, Robert Laffont, 1995), together with two short volumes of collections of his sayings, in both English and French translation: *100 Maxims of Guidance* and

[178] In English, the paperback edition of Corbin's *Creative Imagination* is now republished under the title *Alone With the Alone* (Princeton, Princeton University Press, 1998; with a new preface by H. Bloom).

[179] A number of recordings of musical performances from the last years of Ostad Elahi's life are now readily available in CD format from any 'world-music' retailer or website. Additional helpful biographical references and background can be found on the following closely related websites (all with full English versions) which grew out of the 1995 centenary celebrations: *www.fondationostadelahi.org* ; *www.nourfoundation.com* ; and *www.saintjani.org*. The latter site is devoted to Ostad Elahi's younger sister, Malek Jân (better known today by her nickname 'Jânî'), 1906-1993, who became an influential and highly revered spiritual figure in her own right.

Words of Faith: Prayers of Ostad Elahi (both Paris, R. Laffont, 1995). The volume of proceedings of the international colloquia held in Paris and New York for the centenary includes a number of studies (in both French and English) applying Ostad Elahi's perspectives to a broad range of contemporary ethical and social concerns: *Le Spirituel: Pluralité et Unité* ('Cahiers d'Anthropologie Religieuse', t. 5), ed. M. Meslin (Paris, Presses de l'Université, 1996); it is now complemented by the proceedings of a more recent conference sponsored by the 'fondation Ostad Elahi', *Dieu a-t-il sa place dans l'éthique?* (Paris, l'Harmattan, 2002). (See especially our study of '*L'éveil de l'intelligence spirituelle et les dimensions du processus éthique selon Ostad Elahi*', pp. 86-98.)

Our translation and helpful Introduction to one of Ostad Elahi's key final books, *Knowing the Spirit* (*Maᶜrifat ar-Rūḥ*), an extraordinarily revealing 'phenomenology of the spirit' written for a learned audience familiar with the philosophy of Sadra, should be published in 2004. We have been using several translated chapters from the two-volume Persian record of his oral sayings from the later years of his life, entitled *Āthār al-Ḥaqq* ('*Traces of the Truth*'), in teaching for many years, and hope to begin publishing those translations, which will require a number of volumes in English, in the near future.

Several important new studies developing approaches based on Ostad Elahi's works have been recently published—originally in French, but now available in English translation—by Dr. Bahram Elahi, beginning with a broad survey of his spiritual teachings in *The Path of Perfection* (Shaftesbury, Element Books, 1993). He has since elaborated those ideas, within a broader scientific context, in an ongoing series of lectures at the Sorbonne, published to date in the following three volumes, *Foundations of Natural Spirituality: A Scientific Approach to the Nature of the Spiritual Self* (Cornwall Books, 1998); *Spirituality is a Science: Foundations of Natural Spirituality, vol. II* (Cornwall, 1999); and *Medicine of the Soul: F.N.S., vol. III* (Cornwall, 2001).

آمین